Inside the Cyclist

Physiology for the two-wheeled athlete

From the Editors of Velo-news

Contributors:

Ed Burke

also H.R. Perez and Patrick Hodges

Photos by Robert F. George

A JOURNAL OF BICYCLE RACING

BRATTLEBORO, VERMONT

Published by Velo-news, Box 1257, Brattleboro, VT 05301

Designed by *Velo-news* and Stacy Morse
Printed by Excelsior Printing Company, North Adams, MA.

Contents

Injuries

Questions

Books

Foreword

How many East Germans does it take to win a bike race? Four, some wags say—a coach, a trainer, a doctor and someone to do the pedaling. It might be funnier to Americans if it weren't so painfully true. In modern bicycle racing, especially on the international level, the time is long past when a rider can be successful without steady guidance from experts in training methods and exercise physiology.

During the last several years we have watched cyclists from small Eastern European countries and the Soviet Union begin to dominate amateur racing. Rumors have spread about sports "factories" that can pop out a world champion for practically every Olympic event. It might be accurate in a sense, but only because the sports medicine systems are able to locate potentially great cyclists and then train them to perform at their best.

U.S. cycling is now starting to catch up. Beginning from a void, there has been in the last five years an increasing number of sports physiologists looking into the particulars of cycling performance. During that time *Velo-news*, the nation's leading journal of bicycle racing, has been making such studies available through its pages to riders of all ages, abilities and aspirations.

Readers of *Velo-news* who have been clipping and saving these articles have repeatedly asked that they be made available in a more permanent form. *Inside the Cyclist* is the result—it is a collection of what we consider to be the most important and helpful articles on cycling physiology from *Velo-news* issues through the summer of 1979.

Because the original articles were published in our newspaper format, this book has several visual inconsistencies. One occurs because most of the type was not reset for this volume but recycled, and the *Velo-news* type style has been changed over the years. Additionally, our style on charts and diagrams has been altered. But although the appearance may not be uniform, the information is all there.

Careful readers are apt to also find a few discrepancies among the articles. This is because physiologists, like riders who debate the merits of cycling equipment, can sometimes have differences of opinion. The study of cycling physiology, being as new in the U.S. as it is, will undoubtedly foster much fresh thinking and altered theories in the years ahead, just as it has already begun to do.

Here is your starting point. Whether you are a racer with district, national or international hopes, or a person who rides for fitness and the ability to tour long distances, there is much here to help you perform better. As those Eastern bloc sports systems have shown, there is surprising athletic potential in all of us; it waits only for us to understand our bodies, coax out our strengths, and meet the special needs that will result.

Good luck and good riding. And if you want to stay abreast of new developments in cycling physiology, we invite you to become a subscriber to *Velo-news*.

—The Editors

About the Authors

STAFF

Ed Burke (left), 30, is a former competitive rider who turned his interest in cycling into his major field of study at Ball State University. In the last several years, as he worked toward his Ph.D. in exercise physiology at Ohio State University (obtained in the spring of 1979), he has become America's most prolific writer of sports medicine articles for the cyclist. Burke is a member of the U.S. Cycling Federation's Board of Directors, serving as chairman of its Medical Committee, and he regularly works with national cycling team riders at major international competitions and in laboratory testing. Also, he has been a key figure in conducting USCF clinics for rank-and-file racing enthusiasts around the country.

Several of Burke's articles in *Inside the Cyclist* were written with fellow physiologists at Ball State and OSU.

H.R. (Bob) Perez is a physiologist who administers a program of therapeutic exercise for the aged at Bainbridge (GA) Junior College. While doing research for his Ph. D. at Florida State University, he had the opportunity to work closely with several groups of cyclists of various ages and abilities.

Patrick Hodges, 21, is a Senior I bicycle racer who has competed for four years, winning several Texas district championship road and track medals. His article on carbohydrate loading is an excerpt from a research paper he wrote as a student at Incarnate World College in San Antonio. His major interest in school has been biochemistry and muscle physiology.

Concepts

Some things to know about that pain you feel

By ED BURKE

We have all experienced the pain in our legs at the end of a hard sprint, a fast jam on the road, or an all-out track pursuit. This pain is caused by two nemeses of the hard working rider: lactic acid build-up in the muscles and shortness of breath. Just what is lactic acid? And why do we take such large and deep breaths after the stress, when it seems more logical to breathe deeply during competition when oxygen is needed urgently.

Lactic acid is the end product of anaerobic metabolism, or exercise in which insufficient oxygen can be supplied to produce the energy (ATP) needed to complete the task. The glucose or stored glycogen, which is the only fuel used in anaerobic work, breaks down without oxygen into pyruvate and then to lactic acid (Fig. 1). If sufficient oxygen were present, the breakdown of glucose would proceed to pyruvate and then into the process of aerobic metabolism.

To state it another way, an increase in lactate occurs in an exercising muscle under certain conditions. Work intensity is a major factor, especially in relation to a rider's aerobic capacity. At submaximal workloads (beginning at approximately 60-70% of aerobic capacity) lactate production is found to increase in direct proportion to the work intensity. At very high or maximal work, a constant production of lactic acid is observed (2).

Why It Hurts

At high lactic acid levels, muscular contraction is inhibited. This occurs because of proteins in muscle cells which can function only within a certain range of acidity. Excess lactic acid simply shuts down the reactions taking place within the cells. The result is fatigue, and either the exercise must be stopped or its intensity greatly reduced.

During exercise and for a time afterward , lactate escapes from muscles into the blood, with amounts as high as 20 times the resting level found after extremely hard anaerobic work (1). The exact fate of this lactate is a matter of speculation. We do know that the organ chiefly concerned with its removal from the blood is the liver. There it is transformed into glucose and either stored as glycogen or sent out as blood sugar. Lactate is also picked up by inactive heart and muscle cells which, through a complicated process, use it as fuel.

What effect does training have on a muscle's production of and tolerance to lactic acid? Training increases the cellular components responsible for aerobic work. After training at any submaximal workload, you will produce less lactate than you did when untrained, i.e. your aerobic capacity is greater. Reasons for this are a better ability by the aerobic system to handle lactate's precursor, pyruvate (Fig. 1), and/or the increased use of fats for fuel, which do not directly produce lactate. At maximal efforts, the cyclist will usually be able to tolerate higher lactate levels.

Oxygen Debt

Following a hard interval on the road or a kilometer ride, the demand for energy falls off but oxygen consumption continues at a high level for an extended period. The situation here is "oxygen debt,'' a term misunderstood by athletes who think it is repaying oxygen borrowed from somewhere within the body. Actually, during maximal work, depletion of oxygen stored within muscle and blood would amount to only 0.6 liters. Oxygen debts as high as 30 times this have been found after maximal exercise.

During recovery from exercise, oxygen consumption decreases rapidly during the first two or three minutes, then more slowly until a steady state is reached. The extra oxygen of the first few minutes helps replenish the ATP and PC stores of the muscle, the energy stores used by muscles even before food is used. The increase in oxygen consumption over resting also helps transport lactate and assists in its conversion to blood glucose or stored glycogen. The initial rapid portion of the oxygen debt has been named the "alacticid oxygen debt," and

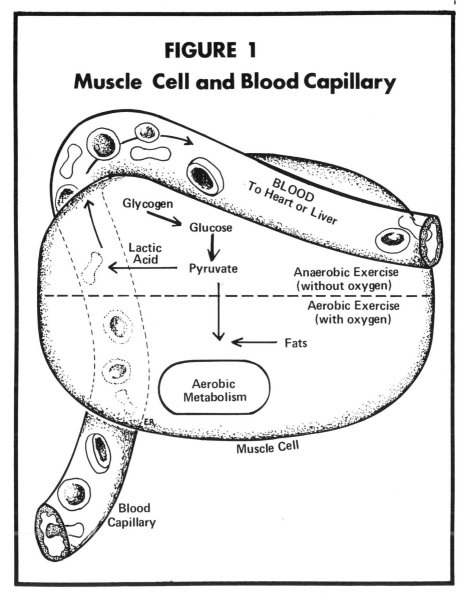

FIGURE 1
Muscle Cell and Blood Capillary

BLOOD To Heart or Liver

Glycogen

Glucose

Lactic Acid

Pyruvate

Anaerobic Exercise
(without oxygen)

Aerobic Exercise
(with oxygen)

Fats

Aerobic Metabolism

ER

Muscle Cell

Blood Capillary

the slower phase is the "lacticacid oxygen debt component" (3).

Have you ever wondered why you were told to keep walking, jogging, or pedaling after a hard effort? During recovery, lactic acid is more rapidly removed and resynthesized by light exercise, rather than by rest. There is a more rapid distribution of the lactate to the liver and other muscles. It is even more important to keep moving when you have to perform several hard efforts and recovery is essential.

References

1. Karpovich, P. and W. Sinning. *Physiology of Muscular Activity,* 7th ed. Philadelphia: W. B. Saunders Co., 1971.

2. Knuttgen, H. G. "Lactate & oxygen debt: an introduction," in *Muscle Metabolism During Exercise,* ed. B. Pernow and B. Saltin. New York: Plenum Press, 1971.

3. Mathews, D. and E. Fox. *The Physiological Basis of Physical Education and Athletics,* 2nd ed. Philadelphia: W. B. Saunders Co., 1971.

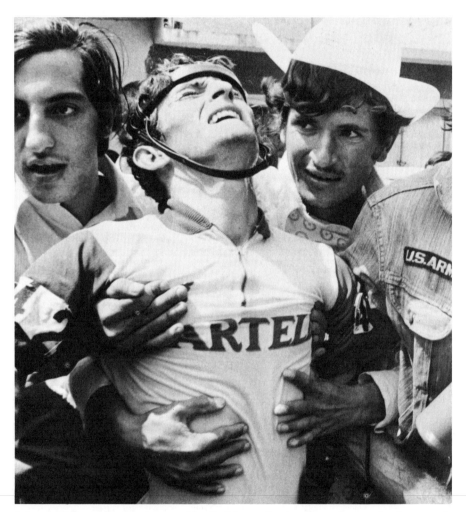

Pain and bike racing are inseparable. But by understanding why you hurt so much, you may be able to train in ways that build both your physical and mental tolerance to it.

Do you have the heart to race with the best?

By ED BURKE
and CARL FOSTER

How many of us have ever wondered what secret is possessed by the Howards, the Mounts, and the Stetinas that enables them to win while we fill the pack or ride the less competitive Category III and IV races. Did they break through the pain barrier during winter training in Florida or Texas while we cursed the snow? Do they know some vague mechanical secret that we have yet to discover? Or do they simply have more of that poorly defined quality known as talent? Our research during the last few years (1, 2, 4) has indicated that cyclists in the better performance categories may possess certain intrinsic qualities giving them an advantage in racing.

The greatest amount of oxygen that can be used during exhausting work (maximal oxygen uptake or aerobic

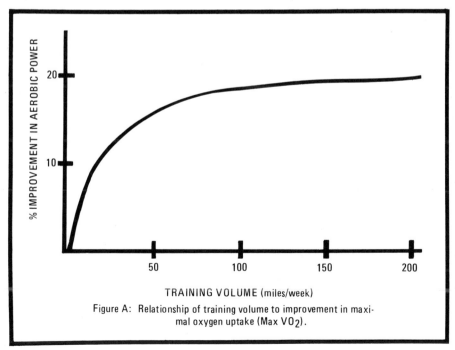

Figure A: Relationship of training volume to improvement in maximal oxygen uptake (Max VO_2).

power) is generally considered the best single indicator of the cardiorespiratory system's functional capacity. The greater the rate of oxygen delivery to the tissues, the greater the rate of work (speed) that can be maintained.

Our research has indicated that there is a steady progression of aerobic power through the racing categories. Since the categories vary in both the rate of work which may be sustained during a race and the rate of oxygen delivery to the tissues, one is tempted to believe that the two may be related. Results from testing support the concept that aerobic power and racing performance are related.

It is well known that aerobic power improves with training. The magnitude of improvement, usually 15 to 20%, is far less, however, than the differences among the categories (25 to 30%). Since aerobic power shows most of its improvement with relatively modest training (Figure A), the greater volume and intensity of training done by the better riders would not be the reason for the differences in aerobic power among the categories.

But we have answered one question by posing another. What factors allow some individuals to develop more aerobic power than others?

The factors limiting aerobic power are still subject to debate among exercise physiologists. However, most agree that the maximal cardiac output (the greatest amount of blood the heart can pump per minute) is a factor of great importance in determining aerobic power.

The difference between individuals with large values for cardiac output and those with more nominal values appears to be a function of the amount of blood that can be pumped with each beat (stroke volume). This suggests that the size of the heart might be inherently greater in some individuals than in others. This is not a startling thought when considering the great size variation of other anatomical features. If tall individuals have a natural advantage in basketball, and large individuals dominate football, why not large hearts

dominating endurance sports like cycling?

Does this mean that unless your aerobic power is above 70 ml/kg you have no hope of riding Category I? The answer is both no and yes. The range of variation within a category is quite large. We have tested Category III riders above 65 ml/kg and Category I riders as low as 60 ml/kg. This certainly proves that relatively great aerobic power is no assurance of success. However, it also suggests that there may be some functional lower limit for aerobic power necessary to break into Category I.

There is relatively great variation in performance for a given individual as more and more training is done, even though that individual's aerobic power may not change. It is known that runners with lower aerobic power may perform at the same level as more "talented" runners by doing a greater volume of training. This suggests that within certain limits, a highly motivated cyclist with less than optimal talent may perform quite well. This secondary training effect is probably due to changes in the muscle tissue, and is currently the subject of much research in exercise physiology.

Competition is a unique portion of any sport. Very often its importance is overblown. By understanding why certain individuals are highly successful and others highly unsuccessful in spite of rigorous training, we may free ourselves of externally imposed standards of success. Hopefully, this will allow us to enjoy sport more on our own terms.

References

1. Burke, E. and B. Fink. "What muscle fiber type are you?" *Bike World*, (May 1975).

2. Burke, E. *et. al.* "Muscle fiber composition and enzyme activities of competitive cyclists," (1976), unpub.

3. Ekblom, B. and L. Hermansen. "Cardiac output in athletes," *J. Appl. Physiol.*, No. 25 (1968), p. 619.

4. Foster, C. and J. Daniels. "Aerobic power of competitive cyclists," *Aus. J. Sport Med.*, (1976).

What muscle fiber typing can tell the cyclist

By ED BURKE, BILL FINK,
and Dr. BENGT SALTIN

It has long been possible to study the respiratory and circulatory variables of exercise, and these studies have had a great influence on training procedures; but until recently our knowledge has been limited by our inability to directly study events inside the exercising muscle. Such a technique is now available and has been used in enough studies to show that it is not only safe, but extremely useful for the physiological information it can supply. In this article we will describe this muscle biopsy technique and discuss some of the results that have been gathered about the muscle fiber composition of cyclists.

For years the only way to gain access to skeletal muscle was through an elaborate surgical procedure. Today we can do this quite simply by using a biopsy needle 3-5mm in diameter. The subject is first given a small amount of local anesthetic in the skin, and a small incision is made through the muscle to be studied. Since the muscle has no pain receptors, the whole procedure is painless. (Subjects usually call the sensation "weird.") The needle is constructed to extract 20-40mg of muscle, which is enough for several biochemical measurements, including those techniques we call fiber typing.

Skeletal muscle contains bundles of muscle fibers (cells), all of which function basically in the same way. That is, when stimulated they contract and develop maximal tension. Nevertheless, muscle fibers can be distinguished from each other.

Muscle Fiber Types

Certain fibers are able to contract repeatedly when stimulated without much fatigue. This type has long been called red fiber because of its high content of myoglobin (an oxygen-storing protein) and its high aerobic capacity. A cell's aerobic capacity is its ability to produce energy at a steady rate for a long time when sufficient oxygen is available to it, and this comes from its having a large number of mitochondria, which are those components of the cell that contain all the necessary oxidative enzymes. Another characteristic of this fiber is that it develops tension rather gradually, reaching peak tension approximately 100msec (0.1sec) after stimulation. Because of this rather slow development of tension, this fiber is also called slow twitch (ST).

The other major fiber type found in human skeletal muscle has a lesser amount of myoglobin, making it look whiter, and a rather low mitochondrial volume, giving it a lower amount of aerobic enzymes. This fiber develops tension rather fast (20-30msec) but fatigues easily. Its traditional name is white fiber, but we prefer to use the term fast twitch (FT).

These two fiber types have different capacities for breaking down glycogen and accumulating lactate; that is, they have different anaerobic capacities. This refers to a cell's ability to produce energy quickly, but for a short time, when sufficient oxygen is not available to it. The FT fiber has the highest capacity for doing this, and is thus able to perform short term, very intense work.

It should be pointed out, however, that there is a spectrum of aerobic and anaerobic potentials within ST and FT fibers. One person's FT fibers may have a greater aerobic capacity than another person's. In a given muscle, however, a person's ST fibers will usually have a higher aerobic capacity than his FT fibers. The reverse is true for anaerobic capacity. The main reason for emphasizing this is that different training regimens can enhance the aerobic or anaerobic capacity of the muscle fiber. Thus, a cyclist trained for long races may have a higher aerobic capacity in the FT fibers of his legs than in the ST fibers of his arms.

The point to remember is that training can increase the metabolic (aerobic, anaerobic) characteristics of muscle fibers, but a change in fiber type based on contractile speed does not occur. We are born either fast twitch or slow twitch.

In an average population the relative muscle fiber composition is 40-50% ST and 50-60% FT. An interesting point is that within the same individual, very small variations appear to exist in fiber composition from one muscle to another. The only muscle that distinguishes itself from all others is the soleus muscle (a calf muscle), which in humans is mainly composed of ST fibers.

Looking into Cyclists

The question arises whether cyclists have a special muscle fiber composition, and whether certain events favor cyclists with special fiber types. Table 1 gives some information about this. The two Swedes, Jupp Ripfel and Curt Soderlund, are both road racers. Soderlund is especially good in time trials and stage races, whereas he is usually weak in the finish. Ripfel, on the other hand, has an excellent sprint and is a challenge to everybody if he can make it to the last 300-400 meters with the lead group. In view of this, it is interesting to note that Soderlund has a very high percentage of ST fibers (73%) while Ripfel has about equal numbers of ST and FT.

John Bare, a U.S. rider, has 65% ST fibers and a correspondingly high amount of aerobic enzyme activity, which explains why he was able to do well in long races when he competed nationally in the early '70s. Similar findings have been obtained for distance runners: the longer the event, the greater the number of ST fibers. Some world class marathoners, for instance, have been found to have over 80% ST fibers. Such runners, however, are usually poor in the sprint (see Table II).

From this information it is possible to speculate about what is "ideal" muscle fiber composition for cyclists competing in various events. It is rather easy to predict what a sprinter needs: a very high percent of FT fibers which with weight and sprint training can be developed in terms of strength and anaerobic capacity.

It is more difficult to be precise about middle and long distance road racers. This is because much of the energy output in cycling is used to overcome wind resistance. Since it is possible to take advantage of drafting, a cyclist with a rather mediocre aerobic capacity and a low percentage of ST fibers may have a good chance to place. This is especially true on flat courses.

From what has been said, it should be clear that a high FT fiber population is a "must" for a sprinter, but too many ST fibers may be a disadvantage for cyclists aiming to be among the elite on the road. A muscle fiber composition of 70-80% ST fibers is ideal for endurance riding, but the only events in which such a cyclist can be fairly sure of success would be long time trials or stage races.

A major question is why a given rider can improve endurance so well while others with the same fiber population cannot. This is surely related to the amount and type of training. However, there is another consideration. Fast twitch fibers can be subdivided into two subgroups: one type can more easily improve its aerobic capacity while the other appears to resist endurance training. To become a champion cyclist, therefore, it is most likely necessary to have as many FT fibers of the first type as possible.

Benefit of Training

Finally, a word about training. Besides improving the central circulation, one of its purposes is to develop the aerobic and anaerobic capacities of the muscle. We know that ST fibers tend to be naturally more aerobic, and FT fibers anaerobic, so we need to seek some pattern of workouts that will con-

TABLE 1

Subject (Age, Ht., Wt.)	Sample Site Arm or Leg	% ST	% FT	Enzyme Activity Aer.	Anaer.	VO$_2$ Max. ml/kg
Jupp Ripfel Swedish Champion (33 yr., 175cm, 75kg)	A L	51 52	49 48	Low High	High High	75
Curt Soderlund Swedish Champion (26 yr., 189cm, 74kg)	L	73	27	High	Low	78
John Bare, U.S. Cat. I (26 yr., 170cm, 70kg)	L	65	35	High	Average	70
Swedish cyclists (Group Average) (24 yr., 182cm, 75kg)	A L	51 (40-64) 61 (48-73)	49 39	Low High	Med. Med.	69 (64-75)
Untrained subjects (Group Average) (27 yr., 179cm, 77kg)	A L	45 (14-60) 37 (13-51)	55 63	Low Low	Med. Med.	42 (32-53)

TABLE 2

Distance (Performance)	ST Fiber %	FT Fiber %	Enzyme Activity Aer.	Anaer.	VO$_2$ Max. ml/kg
Sprinter 1000 meters: 1:08	25	75	Low	High	55
Middle Distance* 50 Mile Criterium 2:00 hrs	50	50	Med.	Med. to High	72
Middle Distance** 50 Mile Criterium 2:00 hrs	65	35	High	Low	75
Long Distance 120 Mile Road Race 4:25 hrs	60	40	High	Med.	80
Time Trialist 50 Miles 1:55 hrs	75	25	High	Low to Med.	75

*Excellent in Sprint
**Poor in Sprint

solidate our strengths and improve our weaknesses.

A cyclist who is predominantly fast twitch will already have the edge in anaerobic capacity; he needs to develop his aerobic ability. The reverse would hold true for the cyclist who is mostly slow twitch.

The last question is the one you have probably been asking from the start: How can you know your muscle fiber composition short of having a biopsy?

True, having a biopsy is the only sure way to know, and not enough studies have been done on cyclists to provide a handy formula such as Dr. David Costill worked out for runners (*Runner's World*, April 1974). Fortunately, however, science doesn't always tell us something new; more often it explains something we already know. Any mature cyclist who has had a variety of racing experience, and who keeps a training diary, has a pretty good idea where his strengths and weaknesses lie. He knows if he is one of the few who are either very fast or long-enduring. Or, if he is like the majority who range somewhere between 40-60% ST or FT, he knows fairly well whether he has

trouble making the distance or sprinting for the finish. In short, he already knows whether he must do more endurance work to develop his aerobic ability or more speed work to develop his anaerobic ability.

We hope that you now have a clearer idea of what it is in your muscle you are trying to train. And if the worst happens, you can blame your parents for not giving you the right kind of muscle to begin with.

References

1. Costill, David. "Championship material," *Runner's World*, (April 1974), pp. 26-7.

2. Gollnick, P. *et. al.* "Enzyme activity and fiber composition in skeletal muscle of untrained and trained men," *J. Appl. Physiol.*, No. 33 (1972), pp. 312-9.

3. Gollnick, P. *et. al.* "Effect of training on enzyme activity and fiber composition of human skeletal muscle," *J. Appl. Physiol.*, No. 37 (1973), pp. 107-11.

4. Saltin, Bengt. "Metabolic fundamentals in exercise," *Med. Sci. Sports*, No. 5 (1973), pp. 137-46.

Muscle fibers of sprinters such as national team members Les Barczewski and Mark Gorski, above, are primarily of the fast twitch variety, while long-distance specialists have more of the slow twitch type.

Cycling physiology needs standardized testing

By ED BURKE

Several years ago Britain's Norman Sheil, now national cycling coach of Canada, brought four young riders into the sports physiology laboratory at Loughborough College. Using his experience he had selected them on a subjective basis, hoping that he could develop them into a world-class pursuit team.

The group was tested on the bicycle ergometer to measure aerobic endurance. One rider showed exceptional potential when compared with the others. After intensive training, guided by Sheil, he became a national champion and achieved international success. His name is Ian Hallam.

Maybe the scientists were lucky—one in four reaching such success would thrill any coach. On the other hand, it is a good example of an intelligent coach using physiological testing to help predict success (22).

Coaches in many sports are finding the results of such testing helpful in the training of their teams. For example, if a cyclist is found to have limited oxygen transporting power then more long distance riding can be prescribed to build up the heart and lungs. Another cyclist, overweight at the beginning of the season, can be correctly advised on how much fat to lose.

Because of the lack of a defined testing program in U. S. cycling, coaches and exercise physiologists are using many different tests to assess a rider's physical fitness and potential. This leads to problems when comparing results with those of cyclists tested elsewhere since often no standardization exists. With this in mind, the following list of tests can be used to accurately measure the physical performance capacity of competitive cyclists. References are included for detailed descriptions and testing procedures. Coaches, trainers and exercise physiologists are strongly encouraged to use these tests to bring about a unified program within the U. S. Cycling Federation.

Many cyclists have asked where testing can be done. Many universities have exercise physiology laboratories and need well-conditioned athletes for research. The Olympic training centers offer physiological testing, and more and more federation riders are being tested at cycling camps in Colorado Springs. YMCAs and private fitness centers are other good places.

The remainder of the article will give brief descriptions of the tests recommended for measuring physical performance.

Body Composition

There is a frequent need to evaluate body composition for purposes of recommending proper weight losses after the winter lay off, setting minimum standards for the season, and aiding physical diagnosis. Body composition can be determined using the underwater weighing technique or skinfold calipers.

The best indicator of lean body mass is the Archimedean principle in which the athlete is weighed both in air and water to determine specific gravity. From this value an estimation can be made of body fat percentage using the equations of Brozek and Rathbun (3, 19).

The determination of the cyclist's residual volume (used to correct total body volume) should be calculated using a helium or oxygen closed circuit method, or the nitrogen washout open circuit method (7, 15). If this equipment is not available, residual volume can be estimated from vital capacity (23, 24). Vital capacity, residual volume, percentage of body fat, kilograms of fat, lean body mass, and total weight should be recorded for each cyclist.

When time or equipment is not available, skinfold measurements may be used to predict body density. The Sloan-Weir graph may be used for predicting body density and percentage of body fat from the skinfold measurements (13, 21).

Lung Volumes

Lung volume determinations measured with a standard bell spirometer or computerized spirometer should include the following: forced vital capacity (FVC), forced expiratory flow in one second (FEV 1.0), forced expiratory flow at 25% and 75% of expiration (FEF 25-75), maximum voluntary ventilation (MVV).

In general, these measurements indicate the total volume capacity of the cyclist's lungs. They indirectly assess the strength of the respiratory muscles to exchange air during a single maximum breath.

Explosive Leg Power

The ability to develop considerable power is a prime factor in cycling success. The term "explosive power" has been associated with anaerobic energy production. Several tests are available to measure it.

The Margaria-Kalaman Power Test. This is an excellent indicator of explosive power (11, 13). The cyclist stands six meters in front of a staircase, then runs up the stairs as fast as possible, taking three steps at a time. Either electronic mats or photoelectric cells are placed on the third and ninth steps, then connected to a timer which measures to the hundredth of a second. The test should be administered several times and the lowest number recorded. Results are reported in power measurements, such as horsepower.

Isokinetic testing. The Cybex II Unit (Lumex Corporation) can be used to evaluate the strength, power and endurance in the muscle groups operating over the knee and hip joints. Extension and flexion movements can be recorded for each limb. The unit measures muscular output at preselected and controlled velocities, from isometric (0 degrees/sec) to fast speeds (up to 300 degrees/sec). Strength is determined by a single extension and flexion of the muscle groups at increasing velocities from 30 degrees/second to 300 degrees/second. Subsequently, a power endurance test is administered with reciprocal contractions for 45 seconds at 180 degrees/second. Measurements are recorded in peak foot-pounds for strength tests and total foot-pounds of work for the 45-second power endurance test (4, 5, 16).

Bicycle power (anaerobic) test. This measures the power output of the cyclist on the bicycle ergometer. After a three-minute warm-up at a submaximal load pedaling at 90rpm, the load is rapidly increased to 7kp (3780kpm), and the athlete is told to do anything to maintain pedal speed (including coming out of the saddle). The test is terminated when the cyclist's pedal rate drops below 75rpm. Total riding time is recorded and post-exercise blood lactic acid can be analyzed if facilities are available (1, 9). This test will give a profile of the cyclist's ability to produce high power outputs for short periods of time, plus his tolerance to lactic acid build-up in muscles.

Cardiorespiratory Evaluation

Aerobic and anaerobic fitness should be evaluated during submaximal and maximal exercise on a bicycle ergometer equipped with dropped handlebars, toe clips and racing saddle, or while riding a road bicycle on a motor-driven treadmill (8, 9, 10, 14). These measurements are valuable in assessing the function and adaptation to training of the circulatory and respiratory systems, plus the utilization of energy stores during prolonged high intensity exercise.

The VO_2 max test measures maximal oxygen consumption and consists of a progressive continuous ride on a bicycle ergometer, with the pedaling rate held constant at 90rpm. The frictional resistance is increased 270kpm each minute from an initial load of 540 to 1350kpm until the cyclist is unable to continue. The test protocol should be as follows:

Minute	RPM	Kilopounds	KPM
1	90	1.0	540
2	90	1.5	810
3	90	2.0	1,080
4	90	2.5	1,350
5	90	3.0	1,620
6	90	3.5	1,890
7	90	4.0	2,160
8	90	4.5	2,430
9	90	5.0	2,700
10	90	5.5	2,970
11	90	6.0	3,240

The second test is designed to simulate actual riding conditions. This requires that the cyclist ride a road bicycle on a motor-driven treadmill at 20mph. The grade is increased 0.5% each minute from an initial setting of 2 or 3% (8). If possible, the following measurements should be recorded each minute: oxygen consumption (VO_2), pulmonary ventilation (V_E), respiratory quotient (RQ), ventilatory equivalent (V_E/VO_2), oxygen pulse (VO_2/HR), heart rate.

Blood Chemistry Profiles

Hematological and chemical profiles of cyclists can be useful in establishing their general state of health and state of training (12). If abnormalities are present, changes in diet, rest and training can be suggested.

Hematology measurements should include hemoglobin, hematocrit, red blood cells, white blood cells, mean cellular volume, mean cellular hemoglobin, mean cellular hemoglobin capacity.

Blood chemistry evaluations include glucose, creatinine and lactate after exercise.

Test of Physical Work Capacity

Many times coaches would like to evaluate the cardiorespiratory fitness of cyclists without subjecting them to a maximal oxygen consumption test. Consequently, techniques have been developed which allow the prediction of maximal oxygen consumption with a fair degree of accuracy, using submaximal exercises and measurement of heart rate. The PWC_{170} test is recognized as simple but functional, using selected work loads to evaluate physical fitness (2, 17, 18).

The test consists of two consecutive six-minute ergometer rides in which the work loads are selected to produce heart rates of approximately 140 and 170 beats per minute. Work loads of 1,080kpm and 1,620kpm should be used for cyclists (this is a setting of 2kp and 3kp at 90rpm). If these loads are too difficult, reduce them according to the rider's ability.

The working capacity is calculated by plotting (on graph paper) the heart rate against work load at the end of each ride. A straight line is then drawn through the two points that intersect the graph's line for 170 beats per minute. The estimated amount of work that corresponds to a heart rate of 170 is recorded as the cyclist's PWC_{170} (6, 20). Another advantage of this test is that it can be administered several times during the season without placing undue stress on the cyclist.

References

1. Baker, S. B., and W. H. Summerson. "The Colorimetric determination of lactic acid in biological material," *J. Biol. Chem.*, No. 35 (1941), pp. 535-7.

2. Bevegard, S., D. Holmgren and B. Joneson. "Circulatory studies in well-trained athletes at rest and during heavy exercise, with special reference to stroke volume and the influence of body position," *Acta Physiol. Scand.*, No. 57 (1963), pp. 26-50.

3. Brozek, J., F. Grande, J. T. Anderson and A. Keys. "Densitometric analysis of body composition: revision of some quantitative assumptions," *Ann. NY Acad. Sci.*, No. 110 (1963), pp. 113-40.

4. Burke, E., R. Bartels, F. Hagerman and S. Nagel. "The results of physiological testing of national class 14- to 17-year-old male and female swimmers," *Swim Technique*, No. 14 (1978), pp. 100-2.

5. "Cybex II testing protocol." Bay Shore, NY: 1975.

6. De Vries, H. A. *Laboratory Experiments in Physiology of Exercise.* Dubuque, IA: Wm. C. Brown Co., 1971.

7. Gilson, J. C., and P. Hugh-Jones. "The measurement of the total lung volume and breathing capacity," *Clin. Sci.*, No. 7 (1949), pp. 185-216.

8. Hagberg, J. M., M. D. Giese and K. B. Schneider. "Comparison of the three procedures for measuring VO_2 max. in competitive cyclists," *Europ. J. Appl. Physiol.*, No. 39 (1978), pp. 47-52.

9. Hagberg, J. M., J. P. Mullin and J. P. Limburg. "Psychological, physiological, and training profiles of national-class American cyclists," Unpub.

10. Hagberg, J. M., J. P. Mullin and M. D. Giese. "Effects of pedal rate on the submaximal exercise responses of competitive cyclists," Unpub.

11. Kalamen, J. "Measurement of maximal muscular power in man," Diss. Ohio State, 1968.

12. Martin, Randolph, W. Haskell and P. Wood. "Blood chemistry and lipid profiles of elite long distance runners," *Ann. NY Acad. Sci.*, No. 301 (1977), pp. 346-60.

13. Mathews, D. K. and E. L. Fox. *The Physiological Basis of Physical Education and Athletics.* Philadelphia: W. B. Saunders Co., 1976.

14. McKay, G.A. and E. W. Banister. "A comparison of maximum oxygen uptake determination by bicycle ergometry at various pedalling frequencies and by treadmill running at various speeds," *Europ. J. Appl. Physiol,* No. 35 (1976), pp. 191-200.

15. Mothy, H. L. "Comparison of a simple helium closed-circuit with the oxygen open-circuit method for measuring residual air," *Amer. Rev. Tuberc.* No. 76 (1957), pp. 601-15.

16. Norris, H. "Cybex Positioning Manual," New York: Lumex, Inc., 1975.

17. Placheta, Z., V. Drazil, J. Rous and A. Novak. "Fitness tests based upon submaximal work loads in cyclists," *Cycling and Health.* Brno, Czech.: 1969.

18. Placheta, Z. and V. Drazil. "Application of long-term medical examination results to the training system of cyclists," *J. Sports Med.*, No. 11 (1971), pp. 52-8.

19. Rathbun, E. N. and N. Pace. "Studies on body composition: the determination of total body fat by means of body specific gravity," *J. Biol. Chem.*, No. 158 (1945), pp. 667-76.

20. Sinning, W. *Experiments and Demonstrations in Exercise Physiology.* Philadelphia: W. B. Saunders Co., 1975.

21. Sloan, A. and J. Weir, "Nomograms for prediction of body density and total body fat from skinfold measurements," *J. Appl. Physiol.*, No. 28 (1970), pp. 221-2.

22. Thomas, Vaughan. *Science and Sport, How to Measure and Improve Athletic Performance.* Boston: Little, Brown and Co., 1970.

23. Wilmore, J. "The use of actual, predicted and constant residual volumes in assessment of body composition by underwater weighing," *Med. Sci. Sports*, No. 1 (1969), pp. 87-90.

24. Wilmore, J. H. "A simplified method for the determination of residual lung volumes," *J. Appl. Physiol.*, No. 27 (1969), pp. 96-100.

Will hard efforts help or hurt young riders?

By H. R. PEREZ

Here is a look into the strain that athletes place on their bodies during competition, especially the growing teenager. Physicians and coaches have often been at odds over how much strain the adolescent body can handle, physicians saying that vigorous competition may be detrimental to health while many coaches disagree.

Since young cyclists often compete against older riders, there is need for some objective information. Do mature competitors, who may possess greater work capacities, hold a physiological advantage over younger riders in long races? Our study represents a select group of Junior cyclists, considered among the best in their 16-18 age group. They may be on our future Olympic teams. It is interesting and beneficial to see how well the organ systems of these young riders function.

Subjects

Twelve cyclists, all considered top prospects for the '77 U.S. Junior Worlds team, volunteered as subjects. Sixteen Senior I-II cyclists, experienced in national and international competition and with an average age of 24.1 years, served as the comparison group. Endurance capacity, lung function and body composition were the variables that were measured and evaluated in both groups.

Findings

The characteristic physical profile of the Juniors and Seniors can be seen in Table 1. We found the Juniors to be generally heavier and more muscular compared with the Senior riders. However, the relative fat weight for the two groups was identical. We speculate that the exercise stress factor in bicycle racing (that is, the amount of energy utilized in terms of caloric expenditure) is similar for both the young and adult cyclists, leading to a similar body composition profile.

Since the fat values were not the lowest that have been reported among endurance athletes, this suggests (1) total body weight may not be a critical determinant of success, and (2) fat weight is less related to successful performance and plays a smaller role in cycling than it does in other sports, such as long distance running and cross-country skiing

Aerobic capacity is considered the most important factor related to endurance performance. We noted a significant difference in the aerobic capacity (how much oxygen the body can process) between the Juniors and Seniors. The Juniors' 7% greater capacity in oxygen consumption (liters/min) indicated that they would be exceptionally adept at handling the physical requirements of long distance road cycling.

The values recorded for the U.S Juniors are, however, somewhat lower than the values reported for some European Juniors (4.97 liters/min). But it should be noted that the American Juniors were tested early in the season when their oxygen transport systems were not fully trained.

Table 1

Mean and standard deviation for the physical characteristics of trained Senior I - II and Junior riders.

Subjects	No.	Age yr	Ht cm	Wt kg	LBW kg	%Fat
Senior I - II	16	24.1	178.6	66.5	58.6	11.7
		2.7	7.2	5.3	4.9	3.0
Juniors	12	17.2	179.9	70.6	62.5	11.7
		.6	7.2	7.2 *	5.9 *	3.9

*P .05 Mean significantly different between Senior I-II and American Junior cyclists.

Table 2

Mean and standard deviation for comparison of metabolic data: Endurance capacity of Senior I - II and Junior cyclists.

Subjects	No.	HR max	VE1/min BTPS	VO$_2$ 1/min STPD	VO$_2$ ml/kg/min	O$_2$ Pulse ml/bt
Senior I — II	16	182.7	134.0	4.28	65.2	23.6
		9	23.0	.34	2.4	2.8
Juniors	12	192.2	146.5	4.63	65.9	24.1
		6	9.8 *	.53 *	3.9	2.7

*P .05 Mean significantly different between Senior I-II and American Junior cyclists.

Table 3

Mean and standard deviation for comparison of pulmonary function in Senior I - II and Junior cyclists.

Subjects	No.	FVC BTPS	TLC BTPS	FEV$_{1.0}$ BTPS	FEV$_{1.0}$ %	MVV BTPS
Senior I - II	16	5.77	7.27	4.71	81.7	181.2
		.89	1.11	.73	7.12	21.8
Juniors	12	5.69	7.09	4.36	72.6	169.8
		.47	.53	.61 *	10.3 *	14.2

* P .05 Mean significiantly different between Senior I - II and American Junior cyclists.

Terminology to aid in understanding the tables

LBW = Lean body weight.
VE= The volume of air exchaned in the lungs per min.
VO$_2$ = The amount of oxygen consumed in liters/min.
VO$_2$ nk. jg. nub. = The amount of oxygen consumed relative to body weight.
FVC = Vital capacity, the maximum amoiunt of air that can be exchanged in the lung with one maximum breath.
TLC = Total lung capacity, the total volume of air that can be accommodated inside the lungs.
MVV = Maximum voluntary ventilation, the maximum amount of air that can be exchanged in the lungs in one minute.
This test is a measure of the efficiency of the respiratory mechanics and musculature.

Results of a study performed at Florida State University in 1977 showed that well-trained Junior riders have physiological capacities nearly identical to Seniors.

The findings relative to aerobic performance indicate that (1) there are definite physical benefits that take place in young cyclists when strenuous exercise is performed and (2) well trained Junior cyclists do not enter Senior competition under a physiological disadvantage.

Excellent lung measurements were recorded for both Junior and Senior cyclists. This suggests that oxygen and carbon dioxide exchange is well developed. It also supports research suggesting that the lungs reach their full anatomical growth and development in the teen years. If this is true and if the intensity of training is less than optimal, the respiratory system may not develop to its genetic potential.

It is known that lung function is not *the* limiting factor in the ability to race at near maximum capacity for long periods of time, such as on a hilly course. But developmental deficiencies can add up, eventually affecting total performance and cycling success.

Summary

First, well trained Junior and Senior I-II riders possess similar functional capacities (endurance and lung). Their body composition measures are also remarkably similar. This suggests that physical training during adolescence is important, especially if the body systems are to continue to improve their functional abilities.

The notion that Junior riders should not ride in Senior I-II fields because they are physically incapable is not supported by this study. Conversely, it suggests that Junior riders of the quality evaluated in this study will do well in Senior competition.

Based on these results, aside from the factors of skill and experience (which were not considered here, yet may be overwhelming), Senior I-II cyclists do not enjoy a physiological performance advantage over well trained Junior riders.

Warm up properly to ensure top performance

By ED BURKE

Coaches and cyclists have asked me how important warm-up is and how it should be done before hard training and racing. Here are some answers, as well as a look at cooling down after the ride.

There are a number of physiological reasons why warming up is beneficial. Besides an increase in speed and force of muscle contraction, there is heightened ventilation, oxygen transportation and blood circulation. With these, "second wind" is more easily achieved and the strain on muscles, tendons and ligaments is decreased.

Astrand (1) states that warm-up will give the benefit of higher muscle temperature and escalate the chemical processes used to produce energy. For every one-degree rise in body temperature, metabolism within a muscle cell will rise approximately 13%. At the higher temperature, the exchange of oxygen from the blood to the muscle will be increased. Additionally, nerve transmission is faster at higher temperatures and both the force and speed of muscle contractions are improved.

Active vs. Passive

There are two types of warm-up: active and passive.

Active is the most commonly used and can be either related to the specific skills of cycling, such as actual riding or using the rollers or ergometer, or it can be unrelated, such as calisthenics or flexibility exercises. Both types will raise the body temperature.

Passive heating by baths, showers and massage have been found to have some benefit for increasing performance. When possible, however, active warm-up should be used even if it is unrelated. Passive warm-up is useful when riding is impossible before competition, such as during a busy track program.

Warm-up should be intense enough to increase body temperature, but not so intense that it will cause fatigue. When you have begun to sweat, you have raised your internal temperature to the desired level.

Length of Warm-up

Obviously, the intensity and duration of the warm-up must be adjusted to the individual cyclist. Better performance results after a session of 15-30 minutes rather than just five minutes.

The effects of the warm-up may last up to 45 minutes. However, the closer the warm-up to the start of the event, the more benefit it will have on performance. The warm-up should begin to taper off 10-15 minutes prior to competition and end 5-10 minutes before the gun. This will allow recovery from any slight fatigue without the loss of the positive effects.

There is also a psychological benefit to warm-up, since it helps you achieve a state of mental readiness. Warming up through related exercises appears to sharpen coordination and awareness, and it will establish a neuromuscular pattern of performance.

Injury Prevention

One of the real values of warm-up is its use as a preventative. It has been shown by Start and Hines (2) that adequate warm-up heads off strains, muscle tears and soreness that would probably occur if you went into full performance cold. Morehouse and Miller (3) state that the muscles most often injured are those which oppose the strong, contracting ones. When not warmed up, these opposing muscles relax slowly, thus restricting free movement.

Depending on the event and weather conditions, you have several things to consider when warming up. For a road race, check the course: Does it start with a steep climb? Is there a prime in the first few kilometers? Will you have a few kilometers to ride easy? Is the weather hot or cold? In a track race, a good warm-up should precede every event. Then put the training suit back on to keep your body temperature elevated.

Cooling Down

Now a brief look at the process of cooling down, which is basically just pedaling easily after the race or hard workout is completed.

Cooling down is done primarily to remove the lactic acid that has accumulated in the muscles due to anaerobic work. Lactic acid is more rapidly removed and resynthesized (in the liver or resting muscle) by light exercise, rather than rest. It is even more important to keep moving when you have to perform several hard efforts alternating with periods of inactivity, such as at a track meet. Otherwise you run the risk of muscle soreness and tightness.

When warming up before a race, start at an easy pace and finish in a light sweat several minutes before the start. Give yourself time to catch your breath and become composed, but not so much that you'll begin to feel cool.

References

1. Astrand, P. O. and K. Rodahl. *Textbook of Work Physiology.* New York: McGraw-Hill, 1978.

2. Start, J. B. and J. Hines. "The effect of warming-up on the incidence of muscle injury during activities involving maximal strength, speed, and endurance," *J. of Sport Med.,* No. 3 (1963), p. 208.

3. Morehouse, L. E. and A. Miller. *Physiology of Exercise.* St. Louis: C. V. Mosby Co., 1971.

Scientific definitions for clinic goers

By ED BURKE and EDWARD FOX

When talking informally with cyclists and other athletes, we often get the impression that there are aspects of laboratory evaluation and scientific terminology which are misinterpreted or misunderstood. With this in mind, and for the benefit of the many riders and coaches who have begun attending clinics given by U.S. coaching director Eddie Borysewicz, here are brief explanations of some important concepts and terms in physiology.

Adenosine Triphosphate (ATP) — A complex chemical molecule formed from the breakdown of food and stored in all cells, especially muscle. This is the last known chemical that is formed prior to the transfer of chemical work to mechanical work.

Aerobic — (Literally, "with **oxygen**.") Exercises which demand oxygen but do not produce an intolerable oxygen debt. They can be continued for an extended period of time.

Alactacid Oxygen Debt — The oxygen consumed after strenuous exercise is used to replenish the ATP-PC energy stores.

Amino Acids — The structural components of protein. There are 20 amino acids of which some are termed "essential," meaning they are not produced in the body and must be taken in with our food.

Amphetamines — A group of synthetic drugs related to epinephrine (adrenalin). Used as stimulants to the central nervous system.

Anabolic Steroids — A group of synthetic drugs that have an anabolic (protein building) effect on the body. Used by some athletes to gain muscular strength.

Anaerobic — (Literally, "without oxygen.") Any exercise that demands so much oxygen that the heart and lungs can't possibly supply it.

ATP-PC System — An anaerobic energy system in which ATP is formed from the breakdown of phosphocreatine (PC). Muscles performing at maximal effort for 10 seconds or less obtain their ATP from this system.

Blood Pressure — The pressure exerted on the walls of the blood vessels as blood is pumped from the heart.

Calorie — A unit of heat. Food and exercise are associated with their ability to produce or use calories. One thousand calories equals one large calorie or kilocalorie (Kcal).

Carbohydrates — An organic compound comprised of carbons, hydrogens and oxygen. Included are sugars, starches, grains, etc.

Cardiac Output — The amount of blood pumped by the heart per minute. At rest, 6-8 liter/minute.

Efficiency — The ratio of work output to work input. Work output divided by work input, then multiplied by 100, equals percent of efficiency.

Electrolytes — Chemicals which ionize in water, such as salt (NaCL). These particles become electrically charged and are referred to as ions.

Energy — The capacity for doing work.

Enzymes — Special proteins which speed up (catalyze) reactions. Each enzyme is specific for a given biochemical reaction.

Ergometer — A stationary bicycle, used for work output. Measures the physiological effects of exercise.

Fast-twitch Fibers (FT) — Muscle fibers that have a contraction rate 2-3 times that of slow-twitch fibers (ST). Also capable of producing higher power than a ST fiber.

Fat — A chemical compound used for fuel, storage of energy, insulation, and protection of organs in the body.

Glucose — A form of carbohydrate more commonly known as sugar.

Glycogen — A sequence of glucose molecules connected together to make the principal carbohydrate storage material in the body.

Glycolysis — The enzymatic breakdown of glucose to produce ATP. The final product in aerobic work is pyruvic acid; in anaerobic exercise it goes to lactic acid.

Hemoglobin — A protein of the red blood cell which enables it to carry oxygen.

Hyperventilation — An excessive increase in the rate of breathing, resulting in the decrease of carbon dioxide in the blood.

Interval Training — A training system in which the athlete undertakes short periods of work stress, interspersed with periods of adequate recovery.

Isokinetic Contraction — The speed of movement is controlled while the

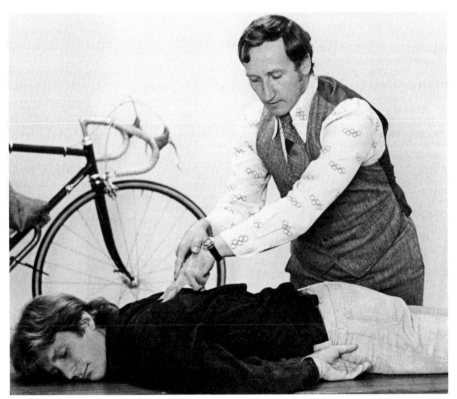

When it comes to understanding the physiology of cycling, few in America can top Eddie Borysewicz. A former national coach in Poland, "Eddie B" is now director of the U.S. Cycling Federation's national coaching program, conducting clinics for cycling enthusiasts around the country as well as national team riders. Above he works with David Ware, twice a U.S. road championship medalist, in a display of massage techniques.

muscle is contracting through its range of motion.

Isometric Contraction — Contraction of the muscle fiber, but there is no change in the length of the muscle.

Isotonic Contraction — Contraction of the muscle fiber in which the muscle shortens.

Lactacid Oxygen Debt — Refers to the oxygen needed after strenuous exercise to remove the lactic acid from the blood.

Lactic Acid — The end product of glycosis (anaerobic) exercise. Causes the pain in the muscle associated with severe exercise.

Maximal Oxygen Consumption (Max VO_2) — The maximum amount of oxygen that an individual can consume per minute. The figure may be expressed in liters of oxygen per minute (L/min.) or, more commonly, milliliters of oxygen per kilogram of body weight per minute (ml/kg/min).

Myoglobin — A protein within the muscle responsible for oxygen transport and storage.

Oxygen Debt — The amount of oxygen that needs to be consumed after exercise in excess of that ordinarily consumed at rest.

Oxygen Deficit — The time during exercise in which the level of oxygen consumption does not equal what is necessary to supply all the ATP.

The athlete is partially supplying his energy from anaerobic stores.

pH — A calculation of the acidic property of a fluid. The normal pH of the blood is about 7.4.

Power — The amount of force (work) expressed per unit of time. For example if one pound is raised 10 feet in one minute, power is expressed as 10 foot-pounds per minute.

Protein — A chain of amino acids which have a specific function (e.g., structure, enzymes).

Respiratory Quotient (RQ) — Calculated as the amount of carbon dioxide produced and oxygen utilized. Indicates the type of fuel being used in the activity. The burning of glucose (RQ=1), fats (RQ=0.7), and protein (RQ=0.8).

Slow-twitch Fibers (ST) — Fibers that contract at a rate two to three times less than a fast-twitch fiber.

Strength — The force that a muscle can exert against a resistance in one maximal effort.

Vital Capacity — Maximal volume of air forcefully expired after maximal inspiration.

Vitamin — An organic material which is essential in chemical reactions.

Work — Application of a force through a distance. For example, application of five pounds through one foot equals five foot-pounds of work.

Training

Training with percentages can produce top form

By ED BURKE

Training programs should involve aerobic and anaerobic workouts because bike racing involves both of these processes. By recognizing which of the energy sources are being employed during a given race you will be able to prescribe the most effective conditioning program.

Table 1 shows the relationship between different cycling events and the primary energy sources being utilized. There are three primary sources of energy available. For sprinters, the most important source is the breakdown of high energy compounds called ATP (adenosine triphosphate, the first-hand energy source for the muscle) and PC (phosphocreatine). One thousand meter cyclists and pursuiters use their immediate source of energy from non-oxidative (no oxygen) breakdown of carbohydrates. Finally, long distance cyclists rely on the oxidative (aerobic) breakdown of carbohydrates and fats for energy.

The use of these three energy sources is dependent on the type, intensity and duration of the training. The energy sources are linked to the particular distance that you ride, thus illustrating the principle of specificity of training.

Some of the percentages in the longer events may seem out of proportion, but think about the event for a moment. In a 100-mile road race lasting 250

TABLE 1

TIME SPENT (IN PERCENTAGES) IN DEVELOPING THE ENERGY SOURCES OF VARIOUS CYCLING EVENTS*

	Performance Time	Speed (ATP-PC strength)	Anaerobic Capacity (Speed and Lactic Acid system)	Aerobic Capacity (Oxygen System)
	Hours & Minutes			
100-mile Road Race	3:55 - 4:10	—	5	95
100-Kilometer Criterium	2:05 - 2:15	5	10	85
100-kilometer Team T.T.	2:10 - 2:20	—	15	85
25-mile T.T.	0:52 - 0:60	—	10	90
25-mile Criterium	0:50 - 0:60	5	15	80
	Minutes & Seconds			
10-mile - Track	20:00 - 25:00	10	20	70
4,000 Meter Individual Pursuit	4:45 - 5:05	20	55	25
Kilometer	1:07 - 1:13	80	15	5
Match Sprints	0:11 - 0:13	98	2	——

* Adapted from Mathews and Fox

Table 2 TRAINING PROGRAMS AND PERCENT-AGE OF ENERGY SOURCES DEVELOPED		
Types of Training	% Anaerobic Capacity	% Aerobic Capacity
Sprint Training	95	5
Acceleration Sprints	90	10
Set Sprints	80	20
Intervals	50	50
Speed Play (Fartlek)	50	50
Repetition Riding	60	40
Continuous Fast Riding	15	85
Continuous Slow Riding	5	95

minutes (4 hrs. 10 min.) 5% would be 12.5 minutes. This is a long time to be using anaerobic sources (ATP-CP, lactic acid-ATP systems).

With work time up to two minutes the anaerobic power is most important; at about two minutes there is a 50:50 ratio, and as the time increases aerobic work becomes more important. Figure I gives in percent the total energy yield from aerobic and anaerobic processes, respectively, during maximal efforts of up to 60 minutes duration for an individual with high maximal power.

Although in some events the anaerobic percentage may be low, anaerobic training should be an important ingredient in training programs since you usually do not have the opportunity to race more than once a week. You need the ability to chase or form breakaways, climb hills and sprint at the end of the race.

Table 1 can be used with Table 2, which lists various training programs involving both aerobic and anaerobic training. You can refer to Table 1 for type of training needed for your event, then to Table 2 for a description of the program to be used.

A question that comes to mind for some cyclists is what to do if you ride several events. You should use a combination of several of the training programs and, when a peak period of the season comes up, concentrate on one or two types of training that will bring top form.

(It is admitted that the percentages are influenced by the observations of the author, even though they are based on the research of others.)

Following is a brief description of the various types of training.

SPRINT TRAINING: Repetition of short sprints as a means of preparation for racing. This means riding at maximum speed, an all-out effort for 50 to 75 meters with relatively long rest periods.

ACCELERATION SPRINTS: A gradual increase from a slow steady pace to an all-out effort: one-third easy effort, one-third medium-hard effort and one-third maximum effort, for about 150 meters. This will increase both speed and endurance if enough repetitions are used. It is valuable in cold weather because you gradually reach top speed, which lessens risk of muscle injury.

SET SPRINTS: A series of sprints, each followed by a "rest" period of recovery riding. For example: sprint 50 meters, medium pace for 50 meters; sprint 50 meters, real slow 50 meters; sprint 75, medium 75; sprint 75, slow 75; sprint 100, medium 100; sprint 100, then begin over when totally recovered. This will develop speed and endurance.

INTERVALS: Riding a series of repeat efforts at a given distance with controlled rest periods. The rests will allow return of heart rate to near normal.

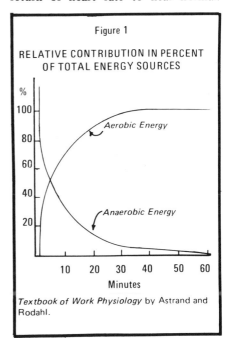

Figure 1

RELATIVE CONTRIBUTION IN PERCENT OF TOTAL ENERGY SOURCES

Aerobic Energy

Anaerobic Energy

Textbook of Work Physiology by Astrand and Rodahl.

Interval training can be divided into two groups:

—1. SLOW INTERVAL TRAINING. Riding repeat distance at slower than race pace with short recovery periods. An example would be 20 x 500 meters with 30 seconds rest in between (a good training pace would be a heart rate of 175-180 beats per minute). This type is used for endurance fitness and does not contribute too much to your speed.

—2. FAST INTERVAL TRAINING. Faster riding pace but longer rest periods which produce a heart rate recovery closer to normal. An example would be 20 x 500 meters with 120 seconds rest interval. A good training heart rate would be 180-185 beats per

Former world sprint champion Sue Novara of Flint, MI, is a track rider who, with changes in her training regimen, can also be effective in criteriums and road races. While sprinting requires virtually no aerobic capacity, a criterium is 80% aerobic.

minute. This helps you withstand fatigue in the absence of oxygen.

SPEED PLAY: This term is used commonly with running (the more common name is the Swedish term "fartlek"). It consists of riding fairly long distances using a variety of speeds. It can be done on a velodrome or on the roads. Basically, speed play uses all of the training methods stated in this article. It is psychologically stimulating, when used properly. An example of a fartlek workout might look like this:

Warmup 5 miles; 5 x 50 meters fast, 60 second rest; 5 miles at ¾ effort; 4 to 6 x 75 meter acceleration sprints (easy 25, medium 25, hard 25, and easy 100 after each); 4 to 6 x 1000 meters faster than race pace, easy 1000 after each; medium pace 5 miles; 8 to 10 x 50 meters at almost full effort, easy 150 meters between; half to three-quarters effort 10 miles; 4 to 6 short hill sprints, ride easy back down; warmdown for 5 miles.

This fast-slow riding is physiologically best for the middle distance to long distance rider.

REPETITION RIDING: Riding a set distance at a fast speed (close to race pace) with rest periods long enough to allow almost complete recovery. Usually the distances are longer than those used in interval training (1,000 to 2,000 meters). The longer the distance the slower the speed. A 4,000 meter cyclist may ride at or near race pace for 2,000 meters with complete recovery between efforts.

CONTINUOUS SLOW RIDING: Riding long distances at speeds slower than race pace. The distance covered will be related to your event. A sprinter may only ride 25 miles, while a road cyclist may cover 125 miles in one training session. This type of training is highly recommended by Dr. Ernst Van Aaken, and may better be known to you as "long slow distance" or LSD. The heart rate is around 150 beats per minute, and no times need be kept. Greatest benefit is in aerobic endurance.

CONTINUOUS FAST RIDING: In continuous fast riding distance is not quite as long as slow continuous riding, but it is longer than race distance. A 3,000 meter pursuiter may ride 3,500-4,000 meters several times, with a 5-10 minute rest period. This type of workout is good for endurance training and it will gradually condition the body to the race pace.

Cycling's Four Seasons

As many of us realize, the cycling season in the United States is long and getting longer every year. A yearly training program may be divided into four areas: pre-season or basic conditioning, early season, peak or racing season, and tapering or rest season.

The pre-season will consist of aerobic training, with gradual increases in speed and distance. Early season continues with a gradual change into anaerobic work. The overload principle is used in training with more intense efforts in terms of speed and total mileage. Speed should be faster than race pace but for much less than race distance.

Peak season may cover several months, and training programs are used to maintain aerobic and anaerobic endurance. Care must be taken to insure adequate rest periods before races. Training pace must be kept high, but at the same time extreme caution must be used not to overwork. Training should be adapted to your racing schedule.

During the rest season you should exercise to maintain general conditioning. It is also psychologically refreshing to get off the bicycle, and participate in other sports. You may ride a bit if you wish (some cyclists have a guilty conscience if they stay off the bike for a few days) but avoid high pressure workouts.

I hope this article has shown you how to plan your season and improve your potential in areas you specialize in. With a little luck the percentages will be with you.

References

1. Astrand, P.O. and K. Rodahl. *Textbook of Work Physiology.* New York: McGraw-Hill, 1970.

2. Mathews, D.K. and E. Fox. *The Physiological Basis of Physical Education and Athletics.* Philadelphia: W.B. Saunders Co., 1976.

3. Wilt, F., "Training for competitive running," in *Exercise Physiology,* H. Falls, ed. New York: Academic Press, 1968.

Train intelligently with a 'profile'

By H. R. PEREZ

Due to confining winter weather, the loss of body tone is an important concern to many cyclists as they begin pre-competitive training. For most, the fundamental questions that now crop up are "How much physical efficiency have I lost?" and secondly, "Which body systems have suffered the most deterioration?" Would it not be advantageous if cyclists had this information early in the season? With it they could program a regimen of workouts that would quickly make up for the detraining of the off-season.

Unfortunately, this information is hard to come by and so the problem is difficult to attack. As a result, the thinking pattern of many cyclists is, "If some training is good, more is better." Even among skilled coaches, who know how to train specific capacities in athletes, there is the problem of knowing which capacities need immediate attention.

Morphologically speaking, each person is different. Road racers and track cyclists differ in body build, and even among road cyclists there exists no common structure. In similar fashion, no athlete gains or loses athletic efficiency according to a specific time table. Also, individual variation governs how optimally an athlete can train.

These points suggest that training effects are gained or lost very quickly. Among individuals that stay fairly active the loss may be gradual, while complete inactivity results in a rapid loss of fitness.

In our 1976 doctoral level study of 16 competitive cyclists at Florida State University in Tallahassee, we performed a host of early season physiological tests designed to assess the functional capacity of each athlete's system. The response of each person's system as it was evaluated during maximal performance was then compared with values derived from the others. This evaluation served to inform the cyclist and coach of the status of trainable capacities, and permits a comparison of similar capacities in cyclists from other parts of the world.

Aerobic Power

Deciding which physiological variables to measure in order to determine the functional capacity of the body's systems is important. Considered first and foremost must be the physical demands of the sport in question.

In road racing it is obvious that endurance is paramount. The relative efficiency of the cardiovascular system (heart and blood vessels) in supplying oxygen to the tissues is closely related to the ability of an athlete to sustain high levels of work for a prolonged period of time. The best index of this is the maximum oxygen uptake, which measures how much oxygen the athlete's muscle cells utilize during the course of strenuous exercise. A high oxygen uptake indicates good cardiovascular function and endurance capability.

In the cyclists tested it was found that the winter lay-off had not produced a great deterioration in the responsiveness of the cardiovascular system to high levels of work. A mean value of 4.28 liters/min (65.2 ml per kilogram of body weight) during February indicates that these cyclists had not been lax during the winter months.

Apparently, engaging in endurance sports such as backpacking, bicycle touring, cross-country skiing, and ice skating is of sufficient stimulus to the cardiovascular system to prevent a serious decline in oxygen uptake from the previous season's high. This means that by knowing his own particular measurement, the cyclist may not have to unduly burden himself with a restricted long slow distance training schedule early in the season. Given an adequate aerobic capacity, the cyclist can begin to concentrate on features of his training program that would ordinarily come later in the season, i.e., pedaling, speed, interval work, bike handling, etc.

Anaerobic Capacity

A measure of an athlete's anaerobic capacity (work without the use of oxygen) can be determined directly by muscle biopsy examination, and indirectly by measuring the speed of muscular contraction during a test of all-out performance. This measure tells how much muscular power an athlete can muster in a short period of time.

Cyclists who are successful in sprint-type, short-duration events generally possess a muscle fiber profile containing a greater number of fast-twitch fibers than slow-twitch. The fiber profile of an individual is genetically determined, meaning that training cannot generate a greater ratio of fast twitch over slow-twitch fibers. Research has disclosed, however, that the potential capacity of each type of fiber can be improved through training. Fast-twitch fibers can be trained by short-term, maximum intensity work, the aim being to maximally engage the contraction mechanism of the fast twitch fibers.

In our study of 16 cyclists a rather low value of anaerobic power was found (55.9 Kcal/ min). Because this was an early season assessment, we attributed this to (1) a lack of sufficient training stimulus (i.e., no interval training), and (2) a general emphasis on endurance training early in the season.

Body Composition

It is generally known that alterations in body weight take place in response to training. What is not so readily apparent is the character of these changes.

Very often a loss in weight is associated with a loss of fat and a gain in muscle or lean body weight (LBW). Unfortunately, this is not always true. Research has shown that weight loss in athletes can often be attributed to losses in both LBW (protein mass) and fat weight. A cyclist who has advance knowledge of his body composition will be better able to organize physical and dietary activities around a program which will optimize training benefits and enhance racing success.

In the 16 cyclists evaluated, an average weight of 66.5kg was recorded. Almost 8kg (17 pounds) of this was fat weight, or weight carried by the cyclists for a negligible return in terms of the energy required to support the extra pounds. Since fat weight contributes very little to optimal performance and in some cases hinders it, riders should take care to maintain a high LBW and a low fat weight — especially when metabolic measurements have shown that it takes more oxygen to completely break down and "burn" fat (approximately 2 liters per gram) than for carbohydrates (approximately 1 liter per gram).

Pulmonary Function

Examining the functional capabilities of the lungs can divulge good information about the efficiency of the respiratory system.

The cyclists evaluated recorded excellent measures for all pulmonary tests, which reaffirm other studies in this area and suggest that lungs do not lose their high functional capacity during short non-training interludes. Therefore, it is probably not necessary for cyclists to undertake specific off-season exercise in order to develop respiratory musculature. Training and competition will have over the years provided sufficient stimulus to maintain the respiratory system in good working order. This is not to imply that this system will take care of itself over an extended layoff.

In order to gain a full appreciation for the values recorded for the cyclists, their physiological profile was compared with data derived from European cyclists (see table). On the whole, it was found that early season values for the Americans compared quite favorably with their European counterparts. This suggests that Europeans are not somehow physically superior to us.

The European Advantage

This profile does not answer why American riders have at this writing (1977) not enjoyed much success in European racing. In fact, physiologically speaking, it indicates that we should. It could well be that a fundamental reason for most of our poor showing overseas is the lack of periodic appraisal of the cyclist's organ systems.

Just as a well-tuned racing car receives constant evaluation before it is put to the test, in similar fashion European cyclists receive periodic progress reports on the state of their body's adaptations to training. These periodic physiological bulletins allow the cyclists to concentrate on any deficiencies that crop up during the season. In several European nations, individual physiological appraisals are conducted on a frequent basis as early as the fifth and sixth year of life!

This has not been the case in our country. Here only the athlete who has established himself as elite is evaluated on a periodic basis. The result is that many individuals who demonstrate good potential never go beyond. In essence, this has been the reason for undertaking this study of 16 cyclists—to provide them a point of reference from which they can begin to measure progress.

If the results of this evaluation have touched any significant conclusions, it points to these factors which should be considered during pre-season training:

1. Detraining does take place during the winter layoff period. This effect can be minimized by engaging in physical pursuits that offer a sporting outlet and present a challenge to the body's organ systems.

2. In spite of all that has been written about competitive training and physiological efficiency, every individual is an entity unto himself. This suggests that every cyclist does not sustain the same degree of detraining in response to a winter interlude. Therefore, an assessment of physiological functions is essential early in the cycling season to pinpoint deficiencies. The net result is a more profitable use of time during training, and a more rapid ascent to competitive fitness with a minimum of internal anguish.

3. The above implies that training programs tailor-made to the athlete are needed in order to obtain optimum results. The construction of a physiological profile is a method of establishing training requirements. This profile can then be used by the coach and/ or athlete to develop individualized training programs which can allow the cyclist to develop to his full genetic potential.

High altitude training and competition

By ED BURKE
and BILL FINK

Ever since Mexico City was chosen as the site of the 1968 Olympic Games, there has been much discussion about the performance which might be expected of athletes training and competing at high altitudes. Of special interest are the long distance events, which require a large amount of cardiovascular adjustment. By the time the 1972 Olympics came along, many outstanding athletes were including altitude training in their programs as a matter of course.

Unfortunately, although there is a wealth of testimony that altitude training has contributed to the success of athletes, the evidence is not overwhelming. Many athletes and physiologists argue that altitude training adds nothing to their performance (1, 3).

Thus, the question is raised: Is the idea that altitude training offers great advantages correct, or is it simply a matter of coincidence that many of today's top athletes either train or live at altitude? A knowledge of the effects of living and training at altitude may help in understanding the part altitude training could play in training programs.

As man travels from sea level to higher altitudes, his maximal oxygen uptake (ability to use oxygen) decreases because the pressure of the oxygen entering the lungs falls, and there is a consequent decrease in the amount of oxygen entering the blood (6, 3). The amount of oxygen in the atmosphere remains the same, 20.94%, but the amount of atmospheric pressure forcing the oxygen into the lungs is less.

At sea level, for example, barometric pressure (standard atmosphere) is 760mm.Hg., but at an altitude of 7,400 feet (Mexico City) the barometric pressure is 580mm.Hg. Consequently, this reduced pressure of the air at high altitudes makes breathing more difficult. The body compensates for the thinner air by increasing its respiration and heart rate in order to maintain an adequate flow of oxygenated blood to the tissues. The only problem is that the extra workload imposed by the increased respiration and heart rate lessens the amount of blood available to meet the energy requirements of the body's other systems (8).

The body, however, is able to adapt to the stresses of altitude if given enough time. This is called acclimatization. It is customary to distinguish between short-term adaptation when it is a matter of days, weeks, or a few months at high altitudes, and long-term adaptation when it is a matter of spending years at altitude.

As the athlete stays at altitude there is an increase in alveolar space (lung size) which allows for more oxygen to enter the lungs. This allows a greater volume of air to come into contact with the blood. There is also an increase in the size of the heart and blood vessels. Another adjustment is an increase in hemoglobin, the substance in the blood responsible for carrying oxygen. The body begins to produce more red blood cells, and this enables the blood to carry more oxygen. The whole effect is a more rapid and efficient movement of oxygen from the lungs to the tissues.

Changes also begin to take place at the cellular level. A substance called myoglobin increases in the muscle cells. It helps carry the oxygen into the cells to be used. The net effect of this acclimatization to high altitude is a *gradual* improvement in performance in those endurance events that require large amounts of oxygen for energy. Nevertheless, all of these adaptations to altitude can also be shown to take place with endurance training at sea level.

From the physiological aspect, then, it is obvious that both altitude training and endurance training produce the same changes, and it is difficult to distinguish between those adaptations that are due to training alone and those that are due to training at altitude.

So what can altitude training offer? The results of research involving the effects of training at altitude and its improvement upon sea level performance differ from individual to individual. Even with apparently well-trained athletes, some investigators have observed improved performance and/or increased oxygen uptake on return from altitude (4), while others have found little or no effects (1, 7, 9). It has been shown by Adams and his associates that runners who are in competitive condition before training at altitude do not increase their aerobic power or performance upon returning to sea level. But even if this is the case, others argue that the athlete may show an improvement in performance by greater anaerobic involvement and by learning to push harder while at altitude. Slight improvement in sea level performances may also be attributed to a general improvement in fitness.

In order to attain top achievement at altitudes of 6,500 feet or higher in activities requiring the engagement of maximal aerobic power, an acclimatization period of no less than three weeks is necessary. A longer stay at altitude would probably be more beneficial from a physiological point of view but may be impossible from an economic standpoint. After an initial acclimatization, an athlete's improvement from week to week is so small that it may be accounted for by day to day improvement in physical fitness (2).

Once at altitude, an athlete should not waste his training time by going easy. In fact, since he will feel fatigued more quickly, he will have to make adjustments to keep the quality of his workouts high. For example, an athlete using fast intervals must take pains to perform them at the same intensity he would at sea level, but he will have to make the rest intervals longer. After all, with a lower aerobic capacity (as exists at altitude) the energy demands of standard work must be more anaerobically provided for than at sea level. This greater anaerobic involvement means that a little more recovery is necessary to restore an equal state of physiological readiness. This suggests that the athlete would benefit more from high quality work than from endurance training.

In looking at all the evidence dealing with altitude and training, we may come to the following conclusions: 1. It is possible to use sea level workouts at altitude, but more quality work should be used; 2. Athletes native to altitude have less difficulty adjusting to sea level than sea level inhabitants have adjusting to altitude; 3. Sea level athletes can improve performance at altitude through a period of training at altitude; 4. Endurance performance times or work output will be better at sea level; 5. Living for an extended period (many years) does produce physiological changes which would help in performance at altitude (5).

References

1. Adams, W. C., E. M. Bernauer, D. B. Dill and J. Bomar. "Effects of equivalent sea level and altitude training on VO_2 max and running performance," *J. Appl. Physiol.*, No. 39 (1975), pp. 263-6.

2. Astrand, P. O. and K. Rodahl. *Textbook of Work Physiology.* New York: McGraw-Hill, 1970, pp. 561-85.

3. Buskirk, E. R., J. Kollias, R. F. Akers, E. K. Prokop and E. P. Reategui. "Maximal performance at altitude and on return from altitude in conditioned runners," *J. Appl. Physiol.*, No. 23 (1967), pp. 259-66.

4. Daniels, J. T. and N. Oldridge. "The effects of alternate exposure to altitude and sea level on world-class middle distance runners," *Med. Sci. Sports*, No. 2 (1970), pp. 107-12.

Anyone who lives at sea level and does some cycling at high altitude will find an initial drop off in performance. It will probably take three weeks of riding to become acclimatized.

5. Daniels, J. T. *The African Running Revolution*, ed. D. Prokup. Mountain View, CA: World Publications, 1975, pp. 40-8.

6. Faulkner, J. A., J. T. Daniels and B. Balke. "Effects of training at moderate altitude on physical performance capacity," *J. Appl. Physiol.*, No. 23 (1967), pp. 85-9.

7. Faulkner, J. A., J. Killias, C. B. Favour, E. R. Buskirk and B. Balke. "Maximum aerobic capacity and running performance at altitude," *J. Appl. Physiol.*, No. 24 (1968), pp. 685-91.

8. Frederick, E. C. *The Complete Runner*. Mountain View, CA: World Publications, 1974, pp. 190-5.

9. Saltin, B. "Aerobic and anaerobic work capacity at an altitude of 2,250 meters," in *Effects of Altitude on Physical performance*, ed. R. F. Goddard. Chicago: Athletic Institute, 1967, pp. 97-101.

Develop lactic acid system for a faster kilo

By ED BURKE

This article is written for the cyclist whose main interest is the 1,000-meter time trial (kilometer). Since performance times are 1:06 seconds or slightly longer, the predominant energy systems used are the ATP-CP system and the lactic acid system.

ATP-CP System

Creatine phosphate (CP), which is stored in the muscle cells, can be used to synthesize the prime energy substance, ATP. Only from the energy released by the breakdown of ATP can the muscle cell perform its work. Activities of about 10 seconds or less performed at maximum intensity derive energy predominantly through the ATP-CP system. The drawback is that both ATP and CP can only be stored in small quantities, though certain training programs can be used to increase storage of ATP and possibly CP.

Lactic Acid System

The lactic acid system derives its name from the accumulation of lactic acid in the exercising muscle, and is associated with painful muscle fatigue. Once the ATP-CP system has been exhausted in anaerobic work, the muscles can continue to produce ATP through the release of energy from the breakdown of food. Glucose is the only food source for this activity. When the oxygen supply is not adequate (anaerobic work), glucose is broken down to lactic acid, allowing ATP to be formed. The lactic acid causes the fatigue, which

is quite real. Ask any cyclist who has ridden an all-out kilometer.

Looking closely at the 1,000-meter time trial we can break it up into several segments. *Reaction to the stimulus* is important in providing a quick muscular movement forward when the gun is fired. *Explosive power* to start the pedals turning in the first few meters combines with reaction time to be an important part of the race. *Acceleration* to maximum speed occurs at different rates in kilometer men, and is generally reached before sitting down. *Anaerobic capacity* dictates how long a rider can hold maximal speed and avoid the slowing that occurs at the end of the race. Any apparent surge of speed at the end of the race occurs only because the rider was not at maximum speed.

The ATP-CP system is used during the explosive power and acceleration parts of the ride, and then the cyclist must depend on his lactic acid system to carry him to the finish.

Some 1,000-meter cyclists have for years used continuous types of exercise in their training. As a result, after several rides, the athlete usually has little energy left to perform a rewarding workout. A number of researchers now believe it better to repeat parts of the total performance, with proper rest intervals, to increase the energy capacities of both the ATP-CP and lactic acid systems.

The cyclist should avoid riding too long in the early season, bringing about total fatigue from the build-up of lactic acid. Hard rides of about 30 seconds or less will enhance the energy stores without substantial increases in lactic acid. As the season progresses, several segments of the ride can be put together to develop the lactic acid system.

Interval training can be used to enhance energy sources and can be approached by:

1. Dividing the ride into segments. This means riding parts of the race independently of each other. This also allows the rider to concentrate more on form, which may save valuable hundredths of a second in actual competition. It is up to a rider whether he will practice one or several segments in each workout.

2. Practicing each part of the ride several times. As the competitive season is coming, you can put two or more segments of the ride together. This will help you increase strength and endurance and the lactic acid-ATP system. You may want to practice some parts on Monday, Wednesday, Friday, and the remaining parts on Tuesday, Thursday and Saturday.

3. Having rest intervals of five to six minutes between rides. This will allow the ATP-CP system to rest and allow for the removal of lactic acid that has formed.

4. Using the rest intervals to work on flexibility exercises or lift weights for upper body strength, which is also needed when riding a kilometer.

Plan your workouts in advance to cover all aspects for reaching a peak at the proper time. Workouts must be worthwhile.

The kilometer rider should know he does not need the endurance of a road cyclist, but must have high anaerobic capacity. This interval training program will allow for the replenishment of ATP-CP for continued work. As you become better conditioned the rest intervals can be shortened, which will allow you to tolerate the build-up of lactic acid. This approach to training will help the specialist train most effectively for the kilometer.

After an explosive start, the kilometer rider must try to hold top speed for more than a minute. The event is often called the most painful in cycling, producing both oxygen debt and a searing lactic acid build-up in the muscles. Pictured is Patrick Gellineau of New York City.

Intervals help heart work more efficiently

By ED BURKE

Interval training is an abused and misused term. Many cyclists believe it to be any fast riding that is interspersed with rest periods. This is incorrect. To understand what interval training actually is and how it affects preparation for various events, let's begin with definitions by several experts.

In their book *Interval Training*, Fox and Mathews describe it as a series of repeated bouts of exercise alternated with periods of relief. Light or mild exercise usually constitutes the relief period.

Allen Armbruster, a well known swimming coach, discusses interval training in his book *Swimming and Diving*. He describes it as a training method which employs alternating periods of work and rest. Although other training systems, such as *fartlek* training (Swedish for "speed play"), have employed alternating periods of work and rest, interval training is unique in that there is pre-planned control over each of the variables. This makes it possible to have precise changes in training stress.

Interval training is the ideal method for increasing the efficiency of the heart. Two factors which enable this to happen are. 1. More work can be performed at a higher intensity than during continuous training, and with less fatigue; 2. The stroke volume of the heart (amount of blood pumped per beat) is increased.

The explanation for the first factor is a bit complicated, involving the chemical energy systems of the body, primarily the ATP-CP and lactic acid systems. ATP is adenosine triphosphate, the ultimate energy source for muscles. CP is creatine phosphate, which is stored in the muscles and used to resynthesize ATP.

The ATP-CP system will provide maximal energy for up to 10 seconds. Then during the relief period a portion of the depleted ATP-CP stores will be replenished by the aerobic system. Thus, for each effort that follows a rest period, the replenished ATP-CP will be ready for use.

Interval training will help spare you from developing lactic acid. In the lactic acid system, glucose is chemically broken down to lactic acid when the oxygen supply is inadequate, and ATP is produced. Without aerobic intervals, muscle fatigue caused by lactic acid buildup will soon make you have to discontinue work. The avoidance of fatigue is a way interval training can help you increase the intensity or length of your workouts.

As to the second point mentioned earlier, there is an increase in stroke volume which takes place during the rest interval. This aids transportation of oxygen to the working muscles. During interval training the stroke volume reaches its maximum level many times, thanks to all the rest periods. In continuous riding there is only one rest interval: at the end. *(See figure I)*

Interval training consists of several

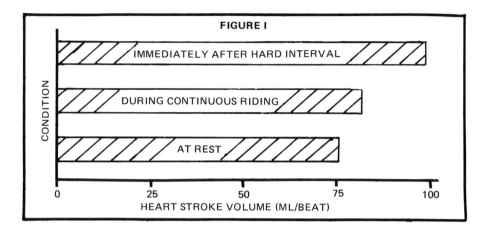

FIGURE I

IMMEDIATELY AFTER HARD INTERVAL

DURING CONTINUOUS RIDING

AT REST

CONDITION

0   25   50   75   100

HEART STROKE VOLUME (ML/BEAT)

variables, each of which can be used to alter the stress of the work being done:

Work period, the portion of the training when hard effort is performed.

Relief interval, time spent between work periods. This may be letting the bike just carry you along, or moderate pedaling which requires some effort. The relief interval can be expressed with numbers, such as 1:2. This ratio means that the length (time) of the relief interval is twice that of the work period. For long work periods the ratio is usually 1:½ or 1:1, going to 1:2 for medium work periods. During short, high-intensity intervals a 1:3 work-relief ratio is prescribed.

Set, a group of work and relief intervals; *e.g.* five 200-meter sprints with predetermined pace and rest periods.

Repetition, the number of work intervals within one set. Five 200-meter sprints would be one set of five repetitions.

Training time, the period for completing the work task. For example, 14 seconds for each 200-meter sprint.

Training distance, the ground covered in the work period.

An example of a written interval training program would be: Set 1— 5 x 200 at 0:14 (0:45). In this formula, the 5 is the number of repetitions, 200 is the work distance in meters, 0:14 is the training time in minutes and seconds, and 0:45 is the length of the relief interval in minutes and seconds.

Table I depicts interval training

programs which can be used to prepare for specific events or situations within a race. This is a basic guideline; you may have to vary this program to fit your personal strengths or weaknesses.

What is Proper Effort?

A question often asked is, "How do I know whether the work effort is too hard or not hard enough?"

There are two guidelines which can be used to determine proper intensity. The first is heart rate response, an excellent indicator. It can be determined by counting the carotid artery pulse (located on the side of the Adam's apple) for six seconds immediately after exercise. Add a zero to put the figure in terms of a minute, and you will have an accurate estimate of exercise heart rate. In high-intensity interval training the pace should be such that the heart rate goes to 180 beats per minute and slightly higher. As the season progresses, the speed at which your workouts must be ridden to maintain a 180 heart rate will increase.

A second method for determining intensity is based upon the number of work intervals that can be performed per training session. At a given work rate, if the full number of repetitions cannot be performed (because of exhaustion) the work rate is too hard. If it seems that additional repetitions could easily be performed, then the work rate is insufficient.

During the recovery period you should keep moving. This will allow a kneading action by the muscles that promotes the return of venous blood to the heart. Keep activity moderate so as to allow the ATP-CP energy system to regenerate. When you wish to stress your lactic acid system, exercise a bit harder between work periods. When doing longer intervals to stress your aerobic (oxygen) system, moderate work should be done during each rest.

By taking your heart rate following exercise you'll have a good indication if you are ready for the next work period or set. A usual practice is to allow the heart rate to fall to 140 beats per minute between repetitions within a given set, and to allow recovery to 120 beats per minute between sets.

Not for Everyday

Interval workouts should not be undertaken more than two times a week for the mature cyclist and once a week for the beginner. Why the caution, you might ask, if interval training offers so many advantages.

The answer is that intervals are hard and there is the risk of injury. Too much work increases the possibility of strain to muscles and joints. Also, the constant repetition of short distances invites boredom or mental fatigue. Cyclists should enjoy the freedom of riding the open road.

Finally, although interval training is essential for some purposes, it does not provide total conditioning or the necessary practice for long road races or long criteriums. Overdistance training and rides close to race pace are needed for further development of muscular and cardiovascular capacity.

Bicycle racing can best be characterized as a fast, continuous activity that intermittently requires periods of great effort. Perhaps you can use the above information to help you better meet this tough double challenge.

Reference: 1. Fox, E. and D. Mathews, *Interval Training.* Philadelphia: W. B. Saunders Co., 1974.

TABLE 1
GUIDELINES FOR INTERVAL TRAINING*

EVENT OR CONDITION (Energy System)	TRAINING TIME (min:sec)	SETS	REPETITIONS	WORK-REST RATIO
Match sprints, starts	0:10	5	10	
jumps	0:15	5	9	1:3
(ATP-CP)	0:20	4	10	
	0:25	4	8	
Kilometer, jams, closing	0:30	5	5	
gaps, team pursuit	0:40-0:50	4	5	1:3
(ATP-CP, lactic acid)	1:00-1:10	3	5	
	1:20	2	5	1:2
Individual pursuit, madison,	1:30-2:00	2	4	1:2
breakaways	2:10-2:40	1	6	
(lactic acid)	2:50-3:00	1	4	1:1
Road, time trials,	3:00-4:00	1	4	1:1
criterium	4:00-5:00	1	3	1:½
(oxygen)				
*Adapted from Fox and Mathews				

Build now for more strength next season

By ED BURKE

You know that the ability to perform well on your bike is primarily dependent upon cardiorespiratory fitness. Most of you put in long miles so that your aerobic and anaerobic energy systems will meet the demands of competition. Rarely, however, will American cyclists possess a level of strength and power equal to their skill level.

The philosophy of many coaches and riders in the U. S. is that resistance training will stifle the smooth motion of the legs, add excess body weight, and work against the suppleness needed to spin at 90 rpm or faster. However, I believe that proper strength training will improve any athlete...male or female, young or old. The better a cyclist is, the more he or she can gain from proper strength training. You will become faster, more flexible, have more endurance, and be less susceptible to injury.

In previous *Velo-news* articles some world class cyclists and coaches have stated that they never use resistance training in their programs. But consider that almost all outstanding cyclists are blessed with superior neurological and physiological systems. To this add cardiovascular endurance training, skill and race experience, and the performance level becomes far above average... even when strength and power may be only average. I think that without exception strength training is mandatory for these and all other cyclists to reach their full potential.

Power and Strength

Before outlining a resistance training program that you can follow in the winter, a definition of power and strength and their relationship needs to be examined.

Strength may be defined as the force that a muscle or, more correctly, a muscle group can exert in one maximal contraction. From this definition it seems that strength may be more important to the weight lifter or shot putter. What benefit does strength have for a cyclist who must contract his or her muscles over and over in events such as the kilometer and the pursuits?

Researchers have shown that muscular endurance is significantly related to maximum strength. If you as a cyclist train to increase your strength, then muscular endurance will increase. The kilometer, pursuits and sprint do require muscular endurance, and imagine how much any cyclist's start or jump could be improved by increasing muscular strength.

Power is one of the most misunderstood terms in cycling. Power is composed of strength and speed, and the formula for calculating it is to multiply force by distance and divide by time.

In the equation, force is the work put into the pedals; distance is the length of the race; time is the duration of the event. You can increase power by exerting more force on the pedals

Table 1
Advantages and Disadvantages of Training Devices

Equipment	Contraction	Advantages	Disadvantages
Free weights	Isotonic	—Equipment is inexpensive —Equipment is generally available. —Specific exercises may be designed	—Workout time is increased with changing weights
Immovable resistance device	Isometric	—Little time involved —Minimal equipment	—Boring —Hard to record progress —Specificity of cycling movement hard to produce
Universal	Accommodating resistance	—Lever system that allows the resistance to change to match the joint's ability to produce a force —Psychologically rewarding	—Expensive —Cannot accurately record weight lifted
Nautilus	Accommodating resistance	—Cam System —See Universal	—Expensive —Plates lifted does not accurately tell force applied
Cybex	Isokinetic	—Exercise can be carried out with maximum resistance throughout the full range of the muscle —Speed can be slow to fast	—Expensive —Exercise movements are limited
Mini-Gym Exer-Geni	Isokinetic	—Inexpensive —Can adapt equipment to specific exercises	—Hard to evaluate progress

or by increasing pedal revolution while in the same gear. Increasing strength is one way of increasing force and power in cycling.

Experience has taught successful coaches that in order to increase the performance of athletes, a specific training program must be planned for their sport. In other words, the resistance training program must work the muscles relevant to the sport. Before proceeding, it is important that several terms be defined.

Exercise Methods

—*Isotonic exercise:* the muscle shortens with varying tension while lifting a constant load.

—*Isometric exercise:* tension develops but there is no change in the length of the muscle.

—*Isokinetic exercise:* a type of training in which the speed of contraction is fixed and the tension developed by the muscle while shortening is maximal over the full range of motion.

—*Accommodating resistance exercise:* training with machines such as the Variable Resistance Universal and Nautilus equipment which allow the resistance to vary during the isotonic movement.

The form of training equipment you can use will most likely depend on what is available. Table I lists the advantages and disadvantages of various training devices. (The availability of true isokinetic equipment is scarce at the present time. In addition to this problem, it is more difficult to define a comprehensive program for cycling because of the limited movements which can be performed with this equipment.)

Table II

Muscles Exercised	Free Weights	Nautilus Equipment	Universal Equipment
Forearm	Wrist curl	Multi-exercise	Wrist curl
Biceps	Standing curl	Biceps curl Compound curl Chin up	Chin-up Curl
Triceps	Reverse curl	Triceps extension Compound extension Parallel dip	Reverse curl Parallel dip
Lower back, buttocks	Deadlift squat	Leg press Squat Hip and back	Leg press
Quadriceps	Squat	Squat Leg press Leg extension	Leg press Leg extension
Hamstrings	Squat	Squat Leg press Leg curl	Leg press Leg curl
Calves	Calf raise	Calf raise Toe press	Toe press on leg press
Stomach	Sit-up	Sit-up Leg raise and side bend on multi-exercise	Sit-up Leg raise
Latissimus dorsi	Bent-over rowing	Torso/arm Chin-up Pullover	Chin-up Pulldown on lat machine
Deltoids	Military press Behind neck press Upright rowing	Omni shoulder Double shoulder	Seated press Upright rowing
Trapezius	Shoulder shrug	Neck and shoulder	Shoulder shrug
Pectoralis	Bench press	Double chest Omni shoulder	Bench press Parallel dip

Strength Program

Your strength-training program should be based on progressive resistance. You will be performing three sets of exercises with six repetitions per set. For each exercise you must determine the maximum you can lift once and perform the following three sets:

1. First set of six repetitions, at 85% of maximum lift.
2. Second set of six repetitions, at 80% of maximum lift.
3. Third set of six repetitions, at 75% of maximum lift.

An example: You can do a maximum lift of 150 lbs. in the bench press, so you would do the following three sets: 1. Six reps with 125 lbs.; 2. Six reps with 120 lbs.; 3. Six reps with 115 lbs. This program will allow you to stress your muscles to the maximum throughout the entire three sets. (Be sure to warm up well and have a spotter handy before trying maximum lifts.)

Table II lists the major muscle groups and the exercises which can be com-

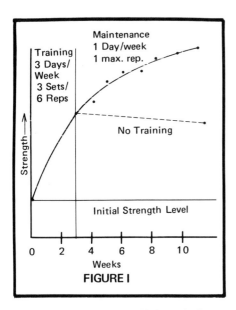

FIGURE I

pleted using Nautilus, Universal Gym, and free weight equipment. The proper technique in performing these exercises can be learned from people familiar with the use of the machines (check the references at the end of this article for specific training manuals). Many researchers and coaches state that gains in strength can be accomplished using any one of the several types of equipment, if the principles of progressive resistance are followed.

When and How Much?

Many athletes are confused about what time of the season to use resistance training and how many days per week they should work out.

Many resistance training programs are incorporated during the off- and pre-season. It is generally agreed that strength and endurance, once developed, subside at slower rates than they were developed. This can be observed in Figure I. There are two important points to note:

First, strength gained during a three-week isotonic training program consisting of three sets at six reps per set, three days per week, was not lost during the following six weeks of no training.

Second, strength was slightly improved or maintained during a subsequent six-week program involving only one set of one repetition of maximum.

This information emphasizes that the most difficult phase of the resistance program is the development of strength and endurance. To then maintain strength you need only exercise once per week or once every two weeks, provided contraction is used. For cyclists this means one upper body session per week throughout the season should do it.

Because there are more and more skilled athletes showing up in cycling, a strength training program may enable you to develop and hold an edge over the competitors in your class, even those who seem to be blessed with more natural ability on the bike.

References

1. Berger, R. "Optimum repetitions for the development of strength," *Research Qtly.*, No. 33 (1962), pp. 329-33.

2. Burke, E. J., ed. *Toward an Understanding of Human Performance.* Ithaca, NY: Movement Publications, 1977.

3. Coker, C. "Universal gym coaches training manual," Irvine, CA: Universal Gym Equipment, 1972.

4. Darden, E. *How Your Muscles Work.* Winter Park, FL: Anna Pub. Inc., 1978.

5. Mathews, D. and E. Fox. *The Physiological Basis of Physical Education and Athletics.* Philadelphia: W. B. Saunders Co., 1976.

6. "Nautilus instruction manual." Deland, FL: Nautilus Sports.

7. Riley, D., ed. *Strength Training by the Experts*, West Point, NY: Leisure Press, 1977.

Ergometer, anyone?

By ED BURKE

Have you ever investigated using a bicycle ergometer as a means of developing your cardiovascular and muscular systems during off- or early-season training?

Ergometers are stationary bicycles used primarily in physiological testing to record accurate work outputs. The frame is solidly constructed and the saddle can be adjusted to your leg length. The handlebars can be exchanged for racing drops and the pedals fitted with clips and straps.

Rollers cannot match the benefits of the bicycle ergometer. While rollers do let you work up a good sweat, they do not allow you to pedal against any great resistance. The work load on the ergometer, however, can be set to provide everything from light resistance to simulated mountain climbing. The load is provided by a frictional band around a front wheel that is driven by pedaling. Resistance can be quickly and easily adjusted by the rider by using the handwheel to change the tension of the band.

By using a bicycle ergometer, performance and fitness levels can be evaluated several times during the season. During testing sessions you may want the help of a teammate to count your heart rate as you ride. This can be taken from the carotid artery (a large artery in the neck located just under the jaw line and beside the Adam's apple). Count the beats for 10 seconds, then multiply the 10-second count by six to determine the pulse in beats per minute.

The use of the ergometer as a training tool can be quite varied. Programs can be developed to include intervals, sprints, strength, and endurance training. Here is an example of an interval training session:

1. Five minute warmup, setting of 2.
2. Five repeats at a setting of 4 for two minutes, with 60 seconds rest between repeats—90rpm.
3. Fifteen minutes at setting of 2.5 at 90rpm.
4. Five repeats at a setting of 5 for one minute, with 60 seconds rest between repeats—90rpm.

On rainy days you may decide to ride the ergometer for one hour at a setting of 2.5. This would be far better than riding the rollers for one hour.

The bicycle ergometer should never be thought of as a substitute for actual on-the-bike training. Technique, form and tactics can only be learned on the road. The ergometer should serve as a complement to the road and as a means of improving physical conditioning and strength. But beware of overdoing it... often riders put in amazing workouts on the ergometer, leaving little energy for the crucial road work.

While there are many ergometers on the market, few are built to withstand the punishment of continued use by racing cyclists. The following two companies have models that seem to be both resilient and adaptable to proper riding position:

—"Monark Bicycle Ergometer" by Quinton Instruments, Dept. E-55, 2121 Terry Ave., Seattle, WA 98121.

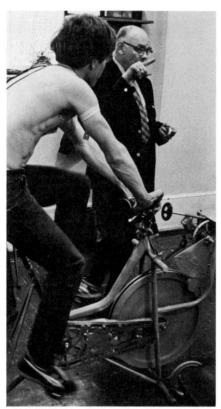

An ergometer has a control to allow precise adjustment of pedal resistance. Such a machine is far superior to the use of rollers, and it permits various training techniques such as intervals and "hill" work. Ergometers are used in the laboratory by physiologists who study athletic performance.

—"Schwinn Ergometer Exerciser" by Schwinn Bicycle Company, 1856 North Kostner Ave., Chicago, IL 60639.

Remember that the seat, handlebars and pedals will have to be changed to adapt these ergometers to a racing position.

The cost of the ergometers ($300-$400) may be prohibitive to individual riders. However, many schools, YMCAs, fitness centers, etc., have units available. Some cycling clubs have purchased an ergometer for use by members.

EDITOR'S NOTE: At the time of his writing, Ed Burke was not aware of the Road Machine, a new home training device that features many of the advantages of the bicycle ergometer, plus some new benefits. For information on the Road Machine, which has a suggested retail price of $269, write: Mechano-Physics Corp., Box 10552, Honolulu, HI 96816.

Also on the market is the Racer-Mate, a stationary riding stand that creates rolling resistance plus wind loads. Retail price for the complete kit is $119.95. For information write to 3016 NE Blakely St., Seattle, WA 98105.

Overtraining:
how to spot and avoid it

**By ED BURKE
and KATERI DAMES**

Exhaustion and overtraining should be main concerns of the bicycle racer. That feeling of fatigue in the last few kilometers is just as crucial as any injury, yet many riders fail to realize that this can be the result of too much training rather than too little. The desire to succeed can make cyclists try too hard in a small space of time instead of pacing and building training; they go too far with the adage, "What doesn't destroy me, makes me strong."

Can the record of the East German and Soviet cycling machines in the last few years be attributed only to the physiological makeup of the athletes? Ability is certainly a contributing factor, but these athletes have shown that top performance must be built through months and years of training with scientifically planned principles.

Physiological and psychological improvement results as stress is placed on your body during training. If your body adapts to stress it becomes stronger; if it fails to adapt it becomes weaker, and an excess of a particular stress could produce a breakdown. By applying the stresses of training sensibly and by keeping alert to the warning signs your body sends, overtraining can be avoided.

In his book, *The Conditioning of Distance Runners*, Tom Osler lists the following danger signs which an athlete's body posts when not responding properly to training:

1. Lowered general resistance (evidenced by headaches, sniffles, fever blisters, etc.) is a sign of physical depletion.

2. Mild leg soreness which occurs from day to day.

3. An "I don't care" feeling toward training and everyday activity.

4. The desire to quit during races.

5. That "hangover" feeling from the previous race and a significant drop in body weight from the day before.

To evaluate the stress of training and racing on your body you should keep a record of your pulse rate. Each morning before getting out of bed count your pulse for 15 seconds; then count it again right after you get up. Do this daily and record the difference between the two rates. If there is a sudden rise in the difference it is a sign your body has not recovered from yesterday's training.

If you haven't recovered, training should either be suspended for that day or done less strenuously. This daily monitoring will give you a general guideline for judging your state of fitness and it'll enable you to better evaluate the effects of cycling and the other stresses encountered each day.

If the signs of staleness are present you may have to spend days or even weeks getting back to the state of fitness you just passed. Therefore, the best treatment is prevention:

1. Do eight to 10 weeks of endurance work to build up a good aerobic base.

2. Sleep at least eight hours a night.

3. Eat a diet which supplies all the basic nutrients.

4. Many coaches recommend a 15-30 minute nap before the afternoon workout.

5. After entering heavy training, speed workouts should be individualized. The appropriate pace is precisely what your own body can handle.

6. Monitor body signs as mentioned above.

7. Immediately before any major competition such as the Red Zinger, lighter training ("tapering") for several days will build strength both physically and mentally for the big effort.

Hans Selye, a researcher, stated in his book, *The Stress of Life*, that every person has only so much adaptation energy to use against stress. If you use much of your physical and mental energy for other matters, you will have less energy for cycling. Consequently, you will not be able to adapt to the stress of the sport. The only way out is to either decrease training or remove or reduce the other stress factors.

Every discussion of stress usually ends with the same definitive statement: too little stress, physical or psychological, does not bring about desired changes; too much is harmful. But by being aware of your body's warning signals and by knowing the stages of adaptation, you can progress in training and steadily improve your fitness.

References

1. Councilman, J. E. *The Science of Swimming*. Englewood Cliffs, NJ: Prentice Hall, 1968.

2. Frederick, E. C. *The Running Body*. Mountain View, CA: World Publications, 1973.

3. Osler, T. J. *The Conditioning of Distance Runners*. Long Distance Log Publication, 1967.

4. Selye, H. *The Stress of Life*. New York: McGraw-Hill, 1956.

Diet

Fuel for endurance exercise

By ED BURKE

Many articles which have appeared in *Velo-news* and other cycling publications have emphasized the role of carbohydrates as the essential ingredient in endurance performance. Besides carbohydrates, fat is also an important fuel utilized by the body in prolonged physical exercise to provide energy for muscular work.

In working muscles we see that carbohydrates are the preferred source of fuel, but as the hard work is continued the supply of carbohydrates is lowered and forces the muscles to derive their energy from fat.

There is some indication that the ability of subjects to utilize fat as a fuel is related to their Max VO_2 (an individual's ability to use oxygen). This may be due to the fact that at a given workload, a cyclist with a lower Max VO_2 will produce more lactic acid (waste products of metabolism) than a cyclist with a higher Max VO_2. High levels of blood lactic acid may interfere with the release of free fatty acids (the form in which fat is utilized in metabolism). It has also been shown that trained skeletal muscle has a greater capacity to use free fatty acids. This increased capacity, combined with the increased ability of trained cyclists to release free fatty acids from adipose tissue, suggests that training enhances the proportion of energy that can be produced through fat metabolism.

In a June 27, 1975 *Velo-news* article, John Allis describes his 1973 Quebec to Montreal race of 170 miles, where he broke away after 10 miles and finished first seven hours later. He was correct in stating that carbohydrate loading could not carry him through a marathon event of this nature. Knowing that John is a highly conditioned athlete with a high Max VO_2, we can assume that the pace he was averaging in the race (23-24 mph) was probably about 70-75% of his Max VO_2. At this pace he was probably able to release and utilize a higher proportion of fats than a cyclist of less ability or training, especially as the miles wore on and his supply of carbohydrates was being depleted.

The question many of you may now be asking is: How do I train myself to use fat efficiently as a source of fuel? The answer is simple. Every time you go out on a four to five hour training ride, you are training your body to burn fat as the main source of fuel as the ride progresses. Also, the highly trained athlete while in a race can ride at a lower percentage of his Max VO_2, which again enables him to burn a higher percentage of fat than the less conditioned rider with a low Max VO_2.

Before you go out and start eating a lot of fatty foods and gaining pounds, remember we are talking about increasing muscle fat and not total body fat. You must train your body to use the fat stores it already has, through distance training and not high fat diets.

Now we can summarize the factors that influence the use of fat as opposed to carbohydrates: 1) The intensity

Carbohydrates are quick energy foods that are fun to eat—fruits, cakes and other sweet things—but remember that your ability to use body fat as an energy source is very important in long distance cycling. Proper training can help this conversion happen after the fuel supplied by your meal has been used up.

of the work in light of the individual's Max VO_2; 2) Duration of exercise involved.

During light to moderate muscular exercise fats play an important role in metabolism along with carbohydrates, but as soon as intense muscular work is started the major source of energy is carbohydrates.

Carbo loading: how it works

By PATRICK HODGES

The growth of sports and attention to physical fitness throughout the world has led to scientific research concerned with the physiological aspects of exercise. This scientific study of exercise, called sports medicine, has made tremendous advances in improving athletic performance.

One area upon which studies have centered is endurance, the ability to resist fatigue. This is a factor that limits an athlete's performance in sports involving high intensity work for long periods of time. Activities such as cross-country skiing, cycling and marathon running fit into this category.

It seems possible that physical exhaustion is caused not only by depletion of glycogen in the muscle, but perhaps it is also due to a failure in the nervous system supplying the muscle. It is well established that prolonged heavy work is usually accompanied by a significant drop in blood glucose levels. Since the nervous system has an important requirement for glucose from the blood, hypoglycemic conditions brought about by prolonged severe exercise may be an explanation for fatigue. If this theory is true, then athletes could possibly improve their endurance by increasing the concentration of sugars in their muscles and blood.

Carbohydrate Loading

Glycogen is the main fuel for working muscles, while blood glucose is a nutrient primarily needed for the proper functioning of the central nervous system. As many recent studies have shown, there is an advantage for athletes in establishing and maintaining high levels of these sugars especially for those involved in concentrated but lengthy activities. The following seven-day program (often called "carbohydrate loading") has been found to be the most effective method of obtaining and maintaining high levels of these sugars.

The muscles are first depleted of their glycogen by intense exercise on the beginning day of the program. For the rest of the week, training is done at low intensity with no real exertion.

Starting with the first day, the athlete's diet is low in carbohydrates and high in protein and fat. Then, on the fourth day, carbohydrates become the main part of the diet with the athlete consuming large amounts of breads, cereal products, and sweets. This high carbohydrate diet is continued to the seventh day, which would be the day before competition.

This technique produces very high levels of muscle glycogen content. Values will reach four grams per 100 grams of muscle vs. the normal amount of approximately 1.5 grams.

Caution is Urged

This procedure should only be carried out two or three times a year. Should an athlete subsist on a high carbohydrate diet regularly, this may condition his metabolic processes to the utilization of carbohydrate fuel rather than free fatty acids. The result is that muscles will not respond to glycogen storage techniques as effectively.

To maintain high levels of blood glucose and prevent the ill effects of hypoglycemia, an athlete should consume small portions of a flavored isotonic solution of glucose, or glucose and some salt, at frequent intervals during competition. If possible, the fluid should be chilled to 46-53F degrees, which will help cool the body. Concentrated sugar solutions should not be used as they tend to create an osmotic effect, drawing water into the stomach and causing cramps. A 5% solution appears to be the desired concentration since the body cannot absorb more than 50 grams of sugar per hour.

For the same reason, an athlete should not ingest excessive amounts of sugar before an event, as is commonly done. The hypotonic condition this creates will surely hurt an athlete's performance more than help it.

Glycogen storage techniques are widely used throughout the world today, and have improved athletic performance greatly. Current research is being directed toward understanding the increased glycogen storage that is the result of such techniques. Perhaps endurance will be further improved when this understanding comes.

In long distance road races or steady touring, the carbohydrate loading diet can pay big dividends. The technique elevates the muscles' stores of their primary fuel, glycogen, helping to make you stronger longer. But research has found that this works best when done occasionally for special events; frequent carbo loading may even be dangerous to your health.

Carbohydrate loading may make dangerous diet

By ED BURKE

The practice of carbohydrate loading has been shown in several studies to be effective in increasing performance in endurance activities and it is used by many cyclists in road racing.

This glycogen supercompensation is accomplished by depleting muscle glycogen with a hard ride lasting two hours or more. For several days following, the cyclist eats a low carbohydrate diet while exercise is continued. This is followed by two or three days of easy riding and a "loading" diet high in carbohydrates. This technique has been shown to more than double the glycogen content of muscle and to increase endurance (1).

There are, however, some indications that carbohydrate loading is not completely without risk. The high accumulation of glycogen in muscle tissues has recently been associated with abnormal clinical findings. It has been reported to produce myoglobinuria (blood in the urine), tightness in the muscles, abnormal EKG's, and increased concentrations of fat in the blood. Further, the long-term effects of carbohydrate loading are unknown and need further investigation.

An increase in muscle glycogen storage is associated with up to three times the normal amount of water being deposited in muscles. This can produce a sensation of heaviness and stiffness. Some cyclists have noted an increase in body weight and a decrease in energy output. While many athletes show increased performances, others have reported leg cramps and a "tied up" feeling.

Recently, carbohydrate loading was used by a marathon runner who later suffered angina-like pain and electro-cardiographic abnormalities (2). This indicates that the glycogen and water deposited in cardiac muscle may place the heart under undue stress. Further, the practice by some individuals of eating large meals to increase their carbohydrate intake has also been shown to put excessive stress on the heart. Certain older cyclists who may be susceptible to infarction should be aware that carbohydrate loading may be a dangerous practice for them.

High carbohydrate diets can induce alteration in various types of metabolism. Recently, the technique was shown to alter the supply and utlization of fat-derived fuels during exercise. As a consequence, carbohydrate diets have come under great scrutiny; evidence has been found linking high carbohydrate diets to a high incidence of cardiovascular diseases (3).

Some athletes, after using the carbohydrate loading technique, have experienced blood in the urine, presumably as a result of muscle destruction (4). Low carbohydrate diets before endurance events and dehydration seem to be precipitating factors. Subsequent depletion of critical biochemical substrates such as glycogen to very low levels results in disruption of the muscle cells' membrane, and myoglobinemia (myoglobin in the blood) results.

The problem is that when myoglobin reaches the kidneys it is apparently toxic and may result in acute renal failure. As urinary output begins to diminish because of the disfunction of the kidneys, there is a buildup of toxic metabolites in the body. To a doctor, myoglobin in the urine, appearing as a dark discoloration, is often a clue of serious muscle destruction.

So as not to cause panic, it is not uncommon after a long hard ride, especially at the beginning of the season, for the urine to appear bloody. But when the cyclist produces gross amounts of blood or myoglobin in the urine a complete physical examination should be sought. Blood and myoglobin in the urine remain a most alarming and mysterious overuse syndrome associated with athletic training (5).

While the practice of carbohydrate loading has been successful for many cyclists, all should be aware of the undesired symptoms and side effects it might cause.

REFERENCES

1. Bergstrom, J. et al. "Diet, muscle glycogen and physical performance," Acta Physiol. Scand., No. 71 (1967), pp. 140-150.

2. Mirkin, G. "Carbohydrate loading: A dangerous practice," JAMA, No. 223 (1973), pp. 1511-12.

3. Ostrander, L.D. et al. "The relationship of cardiovascular disease to hyperglycemia," Ann. Intern. Med., No. 62 (1965), pp. 1188-98.

4. Bank, W.J. "Myoglobinuria in marathon runners: Possible relationship to carbohydrate and lipid metabolism," Ann. N.Y. Acad. Sci., No. 301 (1977), pp. 942-8.

5. Sheehan, G. "Bloody urine: Don't panic, collect a specimen," Phys. & Sport Med., No. 29 (1975).

Should your fuel be plant or animal?

By ED BURKE
and KATERI DAMES

Nothing seems more amusing than to sit at a dinner table and listen to cyclists argue over whether a vegetarian or meat-and-potato diet is better for performance. However, no one can win that argument. There have been many successful athletes using each diet, just as there have been athletes of both persuasions who have suffered from malnutrition due to too much rigidity in their eating.

In order to better understand the nutritional advantages (and problems) of the two main groups, let's look at the caloric, protein and fat content of meals consumed by vegetarians and meat-and-potato cyclists.

We'll use for our example a cyclist consuming 5,000 kilocalories a day to meet his caloric output, and weighing 75 kilograms (165lbs). One hundred percent of the recommended daily intake for protein is 0.8 grams for each kilogram of body weight, or 60 grams of protein. Assuming that the cyclist will eat one-third of his kilocalories and protein at each meal, this would be 1,667 kilocalories and 20 grams of protein at each sitting. Table I is an example of a meat-and-potato meal.

Weight Gain Danger

Examining the meat-and-potato cyclist's intake of calories at one meal (2,128 kilocalories), there is a probable excess of 1,380 kilocalories per day. At this rate the cyclist would put on one pound of fat (3,500 kilocalories) in three days unless more miles were ridden in training. In fact, it is relatively easy to consume excess calories when large amounts of animal fat are eaten. And over half the fat intake is through saturated fat, which recent research says may lead to atherosclerosis. Fat is a necessary nutrient but more should be taken into the diet through unsaturated fats.

The protein requirement for a whole day has been exceeded in this Table I meal alone. While protein is an essential nutrient in the diet, and meat protein contains most of the essential amino acids, any excess will be broken down and used for energy or stored as fat. With the price of meat today this is an expensive source of food energy.

Proteins, complex molecules of about 25 different amino acids, are broken down in the digestive tract by enzymes. They then pass through the walls of the intestine and are carried by the blood to every cell in the body. An adequate source of high quality protein is essential for life.

About Protein

In order to select adequate sources of protein, it is important that you understand the concept of protein quality. Proteins may be classified simply into two categories: high quality or complete, and poor quality or incomplete.

A complete protein contains all the essential amino acids. These cannot be synthesized in the body and must be taken in the diet. Poor quality proteins lack one or more of the essential amino acids.

It turns out that the foods which can

supply the highest quality proteins for cyclists come from animal sources such as beef, pork, fish, chicken, eggs and dairy products. Plant protein lacks some of the essential amino acids.

Fiber is Important
Those interested in the fiber content of their diet will notice that lettuce is the only food in Table I containing a significant amount. Fiber stimulates contraction of the intestine. Diets low in fiber may fail to mix the contents of the intestine. Mixing helps nutrients come into contact with the walls where they can be absorbed.

While the meat-and-potato diet may appear balanced, it may actually lack many necessary nutrients and be high in saturated fats.

Table II shows the caloric, fat and protein content of a naive vegetarian

diet. While the amount of food eaten may appear to be large, it nevertheless lacks 650 kilocalories from the required meal content of 1,667. At the end of the day a cyclist eating this way would be some 1,900 kilocalories below his energy requirement. In a matter of two days he would lose a pound of body weight.

In and Out
This problem of maintaining weight is common for many cyclists who are vegetarians. As a result of the low caloric content of their food, they have to eat almost constantly during periods of hard training and racing. Being high in fiber, a vegetarian diet increases the motility of the intestine, causing food to move through so fast that nutrients may not be fully used. This is why in hard stage racing, where the energy

TABLE I
Meat-and-potato Diet

Food	Kilocalories	Grams Fat	Grams Protein
10 oz. pot roast	818	113	56
1 med. baked potato	180		6
2 Tbsp. margarine	200	24	-
2 pieces bread	140	2	4
1 lettuce salad	20	-	-
2 Tbsp. French dressing	130	12	-
1 slice cherry pie	350	15	4
2 cups 2% milk	290	10	20
TOTAL	2128	176	90

TABLE II
Vegetarian Diet

Food	Kilocalories	Grams Fat	Grams Protein
1 med. baked potato	180	-	6
1 cup cooked carrots	45	-	1
½ cup cooked beans	30	-	2
1 lettuce salad	20	-	-
1 tsp. olive oil	125	14	-
1 Tbsp. margarine	100	12	-
1 banana	100	-	1
1 apple	160	-	-
¼ cup cashews	195	16	6
TOTAL	1026	42	16

A question of many cyclists is whether performance will be better when eating a vegetarian diet or one that includes meat. Since there are champions who have won on whole grain as well as hot dogs, perhaps dietary emphasis should be more on ensuring the intake of whatever foods contribute to a good balance of carbohydrate, protein and fat, as well as essential vitamins and minerals.

requirements may be as high as 7-8,000 kilocalories a day, vegetarians seem to be constantly eating or sitting in the restroom.

A vegetarian diet may also lack essential amino acids found in high quality protein. The vegetarian must take special care to include a variety of whole grains, dried peas and beans, nuts and a variety of fruits and vegetables. Beware that grain products are low in lysine and dried peas are low in methionine, and so are considered low quality proteins. However, when grain products and peas and beans are eaten together, an adequate balance is provided.

Other nutrients such as calcium, iron, and riboflavin (B_2) may be in short supply in a strict vegetarian diet which excludes all animal products. Also, vitamin B_{12} (cyanocobalamin) is not found in plant foods. Lack of B_{12} causes pernicious anemia which has an effect on the blood and nervous sytem. This may be the reason why many strict vegetarians (more accurately called vegans) are converting over to lacto-ovo-vegetarian diets which add dairy products and eggs.

One of the main advantages of a vegetarian diet appears to be the low content of saturated fats and cholesterol. Without getting into the disadvantages or advantages of this, it should be noted that some amount of these nutrients is needed by the body.

The ideal diet for a racing cyclist lies between the extremes shown in Tables I and II. The meat-and-potato rider should cut down on his intake of saturated fats and include more vegetable fats, fish and poultry. The vegetarian should add one egg and two cups of 2% milkfat milk a day to his diet, along with 26 grams of complete protein, 16 grams of fat and 370 kilocalories.

The available evidence does not seem to favor one diet over the other in improving performance in athletes. The choice of the vegetarian or meat-and-potato diet is an individual one, but the mixing of both appears more nutritionally sound.

Reference
1. Whitney, E. and M. Hamilton. *Understanding Nutrition.* St. Paul, MN: West Pub. Co., 1977.

Vitamin supplements: needed or not?

By ED BURKE
and KATERI DAMES

The area where faddism, misconception and ignorance is the most obvious in cycling is nutrition.

We've all heard reports that say the use of vitamins, minerals and other food supplements can give athletes a "winning edge." While the use of many types of drugs is illegal, there are no restrictions against vitamin and mineral supplements. In this first of a two-part article, information about vitamins will be presented along with a look into their beneficial and detrimental effects when used by cyclists.

Vitamins are constituents of food; they are organic in nature and are essential for sustaining life and a healthy body. With few exceptions, the body cannot synthesize vitamins; they must be supplied in the diet or through dietary supplements. Vitamins have no caloric value, but function as catalysts (co-enzymes) in nearly all metabolic bodily functions.

Vitamins are divided into two groups: those soluble in fat and those soluble in water. Vitamins A, D, E and K are in the first group while C and the B-complex vitamins are water soluble. Solubility is important in determining whether the body can store a vitamin or whether it needs to be supplied daily. It also determines its toxicity potential when taken in large amounts.

If an athlete does not have enough B and C vitamins, a decline in performance will be seen in a few weeks. They are needed for the production of energy and they are not stored in the body to any significant degree. When the intake is greater than the body needs, the excess is thrown out in the urine.

Excess fat soluble vitamins are stored in the liver and fatty tissues of the body. If stores have been accumulated over a long period of time, an athlete may get along on inadequate amounts for several weeks.

Much research has been done to determine the vitamin requirements of different age groups and for those in special circumstances such as athletics. The recommended dietary allowances (RDA) for most vitamins have been established by the Food and Nutrition Board of the National Research Council. The RDA is based on minimum daily requirements and it provides for variations in the nutrient content of foods.

Why Are Supplements Needed?

After considering the following points, you may decide to supplement your diet with B and C vitamins to ensure an adequate supply:

1. As a racing cyclist, you probably spend a lot of time traveling. Consequently, you can't always eat a well-balanced diet. In addition, the vitamin and mineral content of restaurant food is often lower due to storage, processing and cooking.

2. During cooking, as much as 50 percent of the vitamins can be lost, particularly those that are water soluble.

3. Racing and training increase the metabolism of foods to produce energy.

This also increases the use of vitamins and minerals.

4. Eating high quantities of certain foods increases vitamin usage. Thiamine (B1) requirement is increased when large amounts of carbohydrates are eaten.

5. Taking certain medicine (e.g. antibiotics) decreases the absorption of vitamins.

6. Some authorities mention vitamin losses through sweat, which may be a problem in hot weather and during hard training.

What then is a safe supplemental vitamin dosage for an athlete in training? Any commercial product which contains 100 or more percent of the RDA of B and C vitamins should supply an adequate amount for a cyclist. Read the labels on products from companies such as Shaklee, Vita Lea, Lederle, Stresstabs and Radiance, and they will give you the needed information. Of course if you are sure you are eating a well-balanced diet then a vitamin supplement may not be needed. And remember that *excessive* ingestion of certain fat soluble vitamins may result in toxicity (this will be mentioned below in the discussion of the particular vitamins).

Vitamin B Complex

The known B-complex vitamins are B1 (thiamine), B2 (riboflavin), B3 (niacin), B6 (pyridoxine), B12 (cyanocobalamin), B13 (orotic acid), B15 (pangamic acid), B17 (laetrile), biotin, choline, folic acid, inopitol, and PABA (para-aminobenzoic acid). The term B-complex is based upon their common source distribution, their close relationship in vegetable and animal tissues, and their functional relationships.

B vitamins are very important in the breakdown and utilization of carbohydrates, and also in fat metabolism. In addition, B vitamins are necessary for the normal functioning of the nervous system. It is for this reason that physicians recommend them for people under stress, and what could be more stressful than a 50-mile criterium?

B vitamins are found in brewers yeast, liver and whole grain cereals.

Vitamin C

Vitamin C (ascorbic acid) is necessary to form collagen, which is a cementing substance that binds cells together. It also helps in iron absorption and in the production of ATP during aerobic work. Recent studies suggest that vitamin C supplements may improve physical performance. Future research may clarify the importance of this vitamin for competitive cyclists.

Important sources are fruits and their juices, especially citrus, and vegetables.

Vitamin E

Vitamin E taken in large doses is claimed to improve everything from endurance to sexual performance. Vitamin E is an antitoxidant, which means it opposes the breakdown of fatty acids and vitamin A in combination with other substances that may become harmful to the body.

Vitamin E is required in such minute amounts that even the worst diet probably supplies all the body can use. It is a fat soluble vitamin and is stored in the body.

The normal daily diet provides about 20-25 units of vitamin E, well above the body's needs. Rich sources are whole grains, wheat germ, and eggs. Excessive ingestion may lead to high blood pressure.

Vitamin A

This is a fat soluble vitamin essential for vision in dim light. It is also necessary to maintain normal health of the skin and mucous membranes. Vitamin A is obtained from the body's conversion of carotene found in vegetables and fruits.

The need for vitamin A supplementation does not appear to be substantiated upon theoretical or practical bases, although Soviet research has suggested that in sports requiring considerable eye alertness, extra A is useful.

Important sources are liver, dark green vegetables, fish, and butter. It would appear that vitamin A supplementation is not necessary in cycling. Bodily stores are available for short term deficiency periods. High doses may cause dry rough skin and painful joint swelling.

Vitamin D

Vitamin D is a fat soluble vitamin, and can be acquired either by ingestion or exposure to sunlight. Some people refer to it as the sunshine vitamin since the sun's rays convert a form of cholesterol, which is present in the skin, to vitamin D. This vitamin aids in the absorption of calcium from the intestine and promotes both calcification of bones and phosphate metabolism.

Vitamin D supplements in an athlete's diet appear to have no positive effects. Excessive amounts of vitamin D can cause high levels of calcium and phosphorus in the blood, which can lead to calcification of soft tissue and the blood vessel walls.

Fish liver oils are a good source of vitamin D.

Vitamin K

This vitamin is necessary for the formation of prothrombin, a chemical required in blood clotting. Vitamin K is also required in the production of glycogen from glucose in the muscle. It has not been shown to improve athletic performance when taken in excess.

Vitamin K is produced in the intestine during the presence of certain bacteria. Yogurt, kefir, and unsaturated fatty acids help increase the amount produced.

Although many studies say that vitamin supplementation is unnecessary, more research is being done. Processing, storage and cooking all have an effect on the food that is ultimately digested, and this may be critical to its nutritional value to athletes. So it may yet be proven that large doses of injected or digested vitamins have a beneficial effect on performance.

References

1. Darden, Ellington. *Nutrition and Athletic Performance.* Pasadena, CA: Athletic Press, 1976.

2. Embree, H. and H. DeBay. *Introduction to the Chemistry of Life.* Redding, MA: Addison-Wesley Pub. Co., 1968.

3. Higdon, Hal, ed. *The Complete Diet for Runners and Other Athletes.* Mt. View, CA: World Publications, 1978.

4. Kirschmann, John. *Nutrition Almanac.* New York: McGraw-Hill, 1975.

5. Marks, John. *A Guide to Vitamins, their Role in Health and Disease.* Baltimore: University Park Press, 1975.

6. Smith, Nathan. *Food for Sport.* Palo Alto, CA: Bull Pub. Co., 1976.

7. Williams, M. *Nutritional Aspects of Human Physical and Athletic Performance.* Springfield, IL: Charles C. Thomas, 1976.

Minerals help govern performance

By ED BURKE
and KATERI DAMES

The need for minerals is a subject sometimes neglected amid the publicity that vitamins receive.

Minerals are considered in two groups: those present in relatively large amounts in the body and those needed only in small quantities (the trace minerals).

The major minerals are those needed in levels greater than 100mg per day. This group includes calcium, phosphorus, magnesium, sodium, potassium and chloride. The trace minerals, on the other hand, comprise 17 substances which have biological functions, though the National Research Council has noted only 10. These include fluorine, chromium, manganese, cobalt, copper, iron, zinc, selenium, molybdenum and iodine.

As is the case with vitamins, minerals are important regulators of physiological processes involved in physical performance.

Calcium

Calcium is present in the body to a greater extent than any other mineral. About 99 percent of it is concentrated in the bones and teeth. Calcium in body fluids exerts a profound effect upon muscular contraction. Some athletes contend that when too little calcium is present their muscles go into spasms. Although scientific research does not document this, calcium deficiency may be one of the causes of muscle cramping. Calcium also plays an important role in blood clotting, along with vitamin K.

There are many foods that are excellent sources of calcium. Dairy products are high in calcium, as are leafy green vegetables.

Phosphorus

Phosphorus is a part of the structure of all body cells and is involved in their functions. It is a component of the high energy compound ATP. It forms phospholipids in cell membranes, as well as part of the structure of DNA and RNA (important in protein production).

A deficiency of phosphorus in an athlete is not likely to occur since it is found in most plant and animal foods. Meat, fish, chicken and eggs are excellent sources of phosphorus. Also whole grains, seeds and nuts, and dried fruits.

Sodium

Sodium is the primary mineral of fluids not contained in cells. It has an important function in electrical balance between the inside and outside of a cell.

Some sodium is lost in sweating, but even under extreme conditions it can be replaced by heavier salting of food or by addition of electrolyte drinks to the diet. In the case of muscle cramping which may be caused by salt depletion, salt should only be replaced in conjunction with adequate fluid intake.

No minimum daily requirement has been set for salt, and athletes are seldom deficient in this mineral since it is found in nearly all foods, especially kelp, celery, romaine lettuce and watermelon.

Chloride

Chloride is found in the extracellular fluids of the body in close conjunction with sodium. Chloride has two major functions: It helps to maintain blood pH levels and it helps the formation of hydrochloric acid for food digestion.

Most chloride is taken into the body in the form of sodium chloride, more commonly known as table salt.

Potassium

Potassium is the principal mineral within the cells of the body. Along with sodium it determines the amount of water held in body tissues. Potassium plays an important role in the function of muscle cells, and a deficiency is associated with muscular weakness and fatigue.

Fruit juices, bananas and potatoes are excellent sources of potassium. Also leafy green vegetables, whole grains, sunflower seeds and nuts.

Magnesium

Magnesium's function is related to the activity of many enzymes and it is involved in muscle contraction and protein synthesis. Magnesium is another mineral which has come under scrutiny lately for its possible role in muscle cramping. But research has yet to conclude exactly what part low magnesium levels play.

Magnesium is present in raw green vegetables and nuts. Also figs, apples, peaches and sunflower seeds.

Iron

Some of the body's iron is a constituent of red blood cells in the form of hemoglobin, while the rest is stored in myoglobin and enzymes. These proteins are important for the transportation and storage of oxygen. A cyclist who has an iron deficiency will feel listless and weak and will look pale. In female athletes this condition may occur during the end of the menstrual cycle.

Liver is an excellent source of iron. Also apricots, raisins, brewers yeast, whole grain cereals, sunflower seeds, lentils and egg yolks.

Iodine

Iodine is an essential component of thyroxin, which plays an important part in energy metabolism and mental and physical development. A diet deficient in iodine causes enlargement of the thyroid gland, a condition known as goiter.

While iodine is present in small amounts in all foods, most Americans receive the amount they need from iodized salt. It is also found in kelp, pineapples, pears, citrus fruits and seafoods.

The remaining trace minerals may also be important in athletic performance. However, little research is available to show their possible ability to increase a cyclist's endurance or energy capacity.

References

1. Darden, E. *Nutrition and Athletic Performance.* Pasadena, CA: Athletic Press, 1976.

2. National Research Council Committee on Dietary Allowances. "Recommended dietary allowances," Washington, DC: National Academy of Sciences, 1974.

3. Smith, Nathan. *Food For Sport.* Palo Alto, CA: Bull Pub. Co., 1976.

4. Williams, M. *Nutritional Aspects of Human Physical and Athletic Performance.* Springfield, IL: Charles C. Thomas, 1976.

Drink up to fend off summer's heat

By ED BURKE

It is not unusual to lose 5-10 pounds of water (a pound equals one pint) during a two-hour bicycle race. As a consequence, rectal temperature may rise to 105F degrees. This overheating and dehydration place severe demands on circulation while reducing exercise capacity and exposing the cyclist to various health hazards.

When racing in a temperature of 80F or hotter, the amount of body heat that can be lost by convexion, conduction and radiation is reduced. The primary method of heat loss becomes evaporation of sweat from the skin, which is influenced by air movement and humidity: The higher the relative humidity, the less efficient is the sweating mechanism.

When the cooling mechanism fails because of dehydration or hot and humid conditions, heat exhaustion or heat stroke results.

Heat Exhaustion

Heat exhaustion is characterized by peripheral circulatory collapse. The cyclist becomes weak and fatigued, and fainting may occur. Sweating is usually profuse, but the body temperature undergoes little or no change. The rider may become nauseated and vomit. Headache and restlessness often accompany this.

Remove the rider to a cool area. If the skin feels warm, cool with fans and wet towels. Force fluids, and summon medical aid if there is not fairly rapid improvement or if the rider gets worse.

Heat Stroke

Heat stroke is caused by failure of the sweating mechanism. It is characterized by rapidly increasing body temperature and unconsciousness. The skin is dry, there is a body temperature of 106F-plus and a rapid weak pulse. Vomiting and diarrhea may be present, and the cyclist will eventually go into a coma-like state.

Treatment is immediate emergency care. Lower body temperature to 102F with cold water spray (45F) and air fans, or place the person in a cold water bath. Give cold fluids orally and immediately remove to a hospital. Keep wetting all body surfaces with cold water or alcohol on the way.

Prevention

Heat disorders can be reduced through: 1. availability of water at all times; 2. acclimatization to heat (gradually becoming accustomed to the hot days); 3. awareness that excessive clothing and severe heat and/or humidity may cause problems.

USCF general rule 2.2.7 states that "passing or handing food or refreshments to contestants shall be at the discretion of the referee" in road races. The availability of water should be unrestricted in races where the course or conditions demand giving handups as soon as possible.

Any rider who starts a road race in hot weather with less than two water bottles is only limiting his performance. Sure, the highly conditioned rider can complete a 50-mile race with very little fluid intake. But why put the circula-

When you wait until you feel like you need to drink, it may be too late. Especially in summer, lost fluid that is not continually replaced can lead to decreased performance and possible serious medical problems.

tory system under more stress through dehydration?

Many world class cyclists ignore fluid replacement and simply allow themselves to dehydrate. But the less conditioned rider should be more cautious on hot, humid days.

Fluid replacement needs to also be used in training sessions. The rider who trains without fluids thinking he is producing a lowered need is making a foolish mistake. Make a conscious effort to drink 4-5 ounces every 10-15 minutes in hot weather training and racing.

What to Drink

With so many fluid replacement drinks on the market it's timely to take a look at what cyclists should be using. To find the ideal drink let's first take a look at the composition of the fluid that riders lose, i.e., sweat.

Sweat is very dilute when compared to other fluids of the body. Thus, during sweating you lose by far a larger amount of water than electrolytes (sodium chloride, potassium, magnesium). The body has such a vast store of these that even the loss of several pounds of water will not deplete its electrolyte supply to a great extent. Also, when exercising for several days in the heat the kidneys can adjust for electrolyte loss by limiting the amount expelled in the urine. A cyclist eating a well-balanced diet should be able to compensate for electrolyte losses due to repeated days of sweating.

Many commercial drinks contain some form of sugar, but the addition of even small amounts can drastically impair the rate of stomach emptying. Anything above a 2% solution (one tablespoon per water bottle) will reduce the rate at which water leaves the stomach; and remember, water is what the body needs immediately. As carbohydrate supplementation during exercise is of secondary importance anyway, the sugar content of drinks should be minimal.

The best drink for the exercising athlete then is *water* (with a small amount of sugar if you desire) because this is what is primarily lost in sweat, and it will leave your stomach the quickest. But remember that any time you add sugar to the drink you risk delaying gastric emptying. So how can all the fluid replacement drinks on the market be right in what they're advertising? To this there is one simple answer: You cannot sell plain water.

Certainly it is best to experiment with the use of any drink during training, not racing. When you find something that works well remember to drink it often.

Acclimatization

The most effective method of heat stress prevention is for cyclists to become acclimated to hot weather exercise. This occurs through a 5-8 day progressive program in the heat, something especially important for northern riders who go south in the early season. Heat acclimatized cyclists have more efficient sweating mechanisms and lose less electrolytes (salts) in their sweat.

Regardless of acclimatization and fluid replacement, a cyclist can add to heat stress with improper clothing. Light colored jerseys will help reflect the sun's heat; dark will absorb it. This is a consideration I've been trying to make for the national team: U.S. riders should be wearing white jerseys instead of our traditional dark blue.

The less body that's covered, the more evaporative cooling can take place. Wearing too much clothing can increase the tendency toward heat stress on the cardiovascular system.

Every cyclist responds differently to various combinations of environmental heat and clothing. Some can tolerate fairly heavy heat loads while others have problems competing in temperatures over 80F. If the temperature is extremely hot (90F-plus, over 70% humidity) riders and coaches should schedule training in the early morning or late afternoon. High humidity places an added strain on the rider because of decreased cooling through sweating—sweat tends to drip off and not be evaporated.

Deaths from heat stress occur yearly in sports and are generally preventable. Principal methods are fluid replacement, acclimatization, proper clothing and monitoring weather conditions. Riders, coaches and race promoters should take careful measures to prevent heat injuries during hot weather.

References

1. Costill, David. "Health hazards during distance running," *Sports Med. Bul.*

2. Fox, E. L. and D. K. Mathews. *Interval Training: Conditioning for Sports and General Fitness.* Philadelphia: W. B. Saunders Co., 1974.

3. Murphy, Robert. "The problem of environmental heat in athletes," *Ohio State Med. J.*, 59, No. 8.

Dreaded bonk is six-headed snake

By ED BURKE
and LORI ALEXANDER

In 1976 at the Olympic Trials there was an interesting conversation among several riders about the causes of the "bonk" in cycling. As these and other road riders know, such exhaustion during very long racing seems to be isolated to the riding musculature, and often takes the form of extreme weakness, emptiness in the stomach, cramping, or any combination of the three. Once the distress is felt, the cyclist is unable to maintain the pace and must give up the race.

Many cyclists are heard to say the sole cause of the "bonk" is lack of eating during the race. While this may be one of the causes, it is the purpose of the following discussion to point out others and to show how they can be avoided. We can classify possible causes of the "bonk" into six areas (4):

1. lack of blood glucose
2. lack of fluid
3. loss of minerals or electrolytes
4. overheating
5. depletion of muscle fuels
6. increased lactic acid levels

Glucose Concentration

It is important to maintain a constant level of blood glucose concentration. Only the blood glucose nutrient can be utilized in sufficient quantities by the brain and nervous system to supply them with required energy. It has been shown (1) that 50 to 60 per cent of the sugar supplied by the liver (a storage compartment for glucose) is used by the brain for metabolism.

In studies by Christensen and Hansen (3), subjects were exercised to exhaustion on a bicycle ergometer. Found at this point were reduced levels of blood glucose. After ingestion of 200 grams of glucose and 15 minutes rest, subjects were able to ride for an additional hour. This suggests that exhaustion in many cases may be a central nervous system phenomenon and not the result of muscle fuel stores *per se*.

As a long race progresses, cyclists eat in an attempt to avoid the "bonk." But the stomach has to work harder during digestion and requires a greater blood supply; this need causes a diversion of blood away from the working muscles in the legs.

Solid food will supply fuel, but nutrients can be supplied in more efficient ways. The cyclist can use carbohydrate super-compensation to load the liver prior to competition, along with sugar solution drinks and high calorie liquid food supplements during the race. Ross Laboratories of Columbus, OH, is now experimenting in this area with two of its products, Polycose and Ensure. Ensure contains 1,000 calories per liter of fluid.

In preparing an "anti-bonk" drink it appears a fluid of less than 2.5% glucose is most appropriate during exercise. About 6½oz should be ingested every 10 to 12 minutes during exercise. At this intake the rate of ingestion approximates the rate of absorption, and the glucose absorbed will allow for maintenance of normal blood sugar levels. If higher glucose concentrations are ingested, the rate of absorption goes down; the advantage of greater glucose concentration is then offset by lack of gastric emptying (6). The majority of commercial replacement drinks contain too much sugar to be effective.

Dehydration

Many cyclists will go into a race of 50 or 75 miles on a hot day with only two water bottles. In such an event a rider may lose from seven to 10 pounds of water weight. Even if he drinks both bottles (approximately 40 ounces) this will replace only two and a half pounds of lost fluid. Such losses put severe demands on the circulatory system, which is approximately 70% water.

When water is lost, plasma has a limited capacity to carry nutrients (glucose, fats, oxygen, etc.) to the working muscle and remove the by-products of metabolism (carbon dioxide, heat, lactic acid, etc.). Although it may be impossible to offset all water lost in sweating, even partial replacement can limit the problems of overheating and minimize the threat of circulatory collapse.

Here are three rules a cyclist should follow while training or racing in hot weather:

—Drink 13 to 20 ounces of fluid 15 minutes before riding;

—Drink several ounces of fluid (6½oz.) every 10 to 15 minutes during the ride;

—Keep a chart on your morning weight and don't allow yourself to get into a state of chronic dehydration. Thirst is not always a good indicator of the need for fluids. You should make an effort in hot weather to drink plenty of fluids between meals and in the evening.

Electrolytes

Sweat is very dilute when compared to other fluids of the body. Table I

represents the concentration of some ions in both sweat and plasma. Sodium (Na) and chloride (Cl) are the electrolytes primarily involved with maintaining the water content outside the cells. These two electrolytes in sweat are approximately one-third of that seen in plasma.

If you lose nine pounds of sweat during a long race or training ride, the body's electrolyte losses would constitute roughly 140-150 mEq. of sodium and chloride. Since the body generally contains 2,600 mEq., these losses would decrease the body's total NaCl content by 6-8%. At the same time, the potassium and magnesium losses would lower the body's content by less than 1%. It has been hypothesized that these losses may cause muscle cramps and intolerance to heat.

When sweating at a high rate, more water is removed from the body than electrolytes, causing the electrolyte concentration to become higher. Therefore, in heavy exercise the need to replace body water is greater than the immediate demands for electrolytes (5).

When exercising in the heat for several days, the kidneys can adjust to loss of electrolytes from sweating. This is accomplished through conserving the amount lost in the urine. There seems to be enough evidence available to say that a cyclist on a well balanced diet, who salts his food, can adequately compensate for the electrolytes lost in repeated days of sweating. Replacement drinks may be of benefit at this time to help replenish the lost electrolytes.

Hyperthermia

Even under mild weather conditions (e.g. 70F degrees, some cloud cover, and little humidity) the risk of overheating is a great threat to the racing cyclist. Nevertheless, distance races are frequently conducted under more severe conditions. For example, at the 1974 World Championships the team time trial

Table I
Electrolytes (mEq/liter)

	Sodium	Chloride	Potassium	Magnesium	Total
Plasma	140	100	4	1.5	245.5
Sweat	40-60	30-50	4-5	1.5-5	75.5-120

was held on a day with the temperature over 85F degrees, high humidity and no cloud cover. Not all the teams survived the effort and the heat; New Zealand and Denmark dropped out and one Russian collapsed after the race and was removed by ambulance. Many of the riders showed signs of heat exhaustion (Table II).

Again, the circulatory system is important in the control of body temperature. As the cyclist is riding, the food he has consumed is being converted into fuel stores which can be converted into energy for muscular contraction. At the same time a tremendous amount of heat is being produced. Proof of this is seen when rectal temperatures of 104F degrees or higher are recorded after a long, hard ride.

One primary responsibility of the circulatory system is to transport heat generated by muscles to the surface of the body, where it can be transferred to the environment by sweating and evaporation. There is a transfer of blood to the skin to aid in thermal regulation, although the rider is still in need of large blood quantities for the working muscles. This situation may put severe stress on the circulatory system, causing muscular exhaustion due to inadequate removal of body heat.

The problems associated with distance cycling and running are the same. In work done at the Human Performance Laboratory at Ball State University, it was found that consuming fluids during a two hour run will significantly benefit the runner. Rectal temperatures were 2F degrees lower when runners drank fluids than when they did not. (One

athlete's internal temperature reached 105.5F degrees without fluid intake during exercise and leveled at 103.6 degrees when he drank fluids.) Since a body temperature above 104.5F degrees can cause great stress, the cooling quality of ingested fluids can be of paramount value on a hot day. This is why ingestion of fluids before and at frequent intervals during a long event is recommended.

The heat-acclimatized person will be able to work in the heat with lower rectal temperatures and heart rate, a better regulation of body temperature, and fewer heat stress symptoms than an unacclimatized person. The end result appears to be a greater ability to maintain adequate circulatory function. Acclimatization may be accomplished in four to seven days, with short periods (two to four hours daily) of work in the heat. Exposure to the heat without exercise results in only slight acclimatization.

Muscle Glycogen Depletion

Studies by Hermansen and co-workers show that when trained subjects had exercised to exhaustion in an hour and a half, their thigh muscle glycogen content was near zero (7). The average oxygen uptake of the subjects was about 80% of their maximal aerobic power. This experiment indicates that the initial glycogen content in skeletal muscles is important to the performance of exhaustive work.

The extent that diet affects glycogen stores was investigated by Bergstrom, *et al* (2),using nine subjects. After a normal diet the muscle glycogen stores were

Table II
Correlation of Cyclists' Symptoms
With Rectal Temperatures

Rectal Temperature	*Symptoms*
104-105°F	Throbbing pressure in the temples, cold sensation over trunk
105-106°F	Muscular weakness, disorientation, and loss of postural equilibrium
Above 106°F	Diminished sweating, loss of consciousness

1.75g per 100g of muscle, and the subjects could average 75% of their maximal oxygen uptake for 115 minutes. After the subjects spent three days on a high fat diet, the muscle glycogen stores were 0.6g/100g of muscle and the workload could be performed for only 60 minutes. After three days of a high carbohydrate diet the subjects' glycogen content became higher, 3.5g/100g of muscle, and they could work for 170 minutes at 75% of maximal oxygen uptake.

In further experiments by the researchers, the highest levels of muscle glycogen were observed after subjects performed a heavy workout followed by a low carbohydrate diet for a few days, then by a carbohydrate-rich diet. The muscle glycogen content could exceed 4g/100g of muscle, and the workload could be tolerated in some subjects for up to four hours (1). During heavy work the major source of energy is glycogen.

Role of Fat

During moderate muscular work, energy is supplied to active muscles by fat and glycogen in approximately equal amounts. As work continues, fat increasingly contributes to the production of muscular effort (important in long road races). You are training yourself to use fats efficiently for fuel every time you go out on a ride of 4-6 hours.

In a race, the highly trained cyclist can ride at a lower percentage of his maximal oxygen uptake. This will enable him to burn a higher percentage of fat (and conserve glycogen for hard efforts) than can the less conditioned rider.

This increased capacity of trained cyclists to utilize fats, combined with their ability to release free fatty acids from adipose tissue, suggests that training enhances the proportion of energy that can be produced through fat metabolism.

Lactic Acid Accumulation

Lactic acid is the by-product of anaerobic metabolism, better known as exercise performed with an inadequate supply of oxygen. We have all felt that pain or burning sensation in our legs at the end of a jam, the top of a climb, or after a sprint. The lactate build-up can be tolerated for short periods, but it must be followed by exercise of less intensity to allow the lactate to diffuse from the muscle and be carried by the blood system for disposal in the liver. Because of its ability to be removed from the working muscles, lactic acid accumulation is not the cause of exhaustion experienced in long road races.

Everyone has experienced soreness that results from the extra work performed by muscles. Several theories have been postulated about this. The pain could be associated with injuries to the connective tissue within the muscle itself and its attachment to the tendon. Excessive fluid accumulation might account for muscle swelling to such an extent that pressure would sensitize nerve endings (6).

The painful cramp that puts a working muscle into involuntary contraction cannot be explained at the present time. Stretching the muscle usually relieves the contraction within a few seconds.

References

1. Astrand, P-O. and K. Rodahl. *Textbook of Work Physiology.* New York: McGraw-Hill, 1970.

2. Bergstrom, J., L. Hermansen, E. Hultman and B. Saltin. "Muscle glycogen and physical performance," *Acta Physiol. Scand.,* No. 7 (1967), p. 140.

3. Christensen, E. H. and O. Hansen. "Arbeitsfahigkeit und ekrankrung." *Skand. Arch. Physiol.,* No. 81 (1939), p. 160.

4. Costill, D. L. "Muscular exhaustion during distance running," *Phys. and Sports Med.,* No. 10 (1974), p. 36.

5. Costill, D. L. "Fluids for athletic performance." Unpub.

6. Edington, D. W. and V. R. Edgerton. *The Biology of Physical Activity.* Boston: Houghton Mifflin, 1976.

7. Hermansen, L., E. Hultman and B. Saltin. "Muscle glycogen during prolonged severe exercise," *Acta. Physiol. Scand.,* No. 71 (1967), p. 129.

Too fat? Testing of top U.S. riders gives guide

By ED BURKE

In 1977 at the Junior national training camp in Tallahassee, FL, and at the Olympic Training Center in Squaw Valley, CA, body composition work was conducted on many high caliber U.S. cyclists. With the information gained through this research, a profile of total body fat and body density in national class riders is now available. This can be useful in helping the thousands of other USCF riders know how they compare to the country's best in terms of the fat they are carrying.

The percentage of body fat was determined using the Archimedean principle, in which the athlete is weighed in both air and water to determine his or her specific gravity. Body composition is then divided into two categories: lean body weight and stored fat. Lean body weight (LBW) includes all of the body tissues (muscles, bones, nerves, etc.) except fat.

Most changes in body weight are due to changes in fat content, while LBW remains relatively constant. Men and women training for sports will tend to have less fat than untrained individuals. In the U.S. the average male has approximately 18-21% body fat with the female at 21-23%.

Extensive studies of many different athletes have shown the following body fat averages in various sports: college football, 15%; professional football, 17%; college wrestling, 9%; distance running, 4%; professional baseball, 14%; college swimming, 8%; college gymnastics, 5%; elite heavyweight crew, 11% and elite lightweight crew, 8.5%. (1)

Table I reports on the data collected earlier this year at the Exercise Physiology Laboratory of Florida State University on the Juniors invited to the training camp. While the mean of 11.1% body fat may seem a little high for endurance trained athletes, remember these measurements were made in early season (March) when the cyclists were probably not in top form. Also the average age for the group was 17, and some may have not yet reached full body maturity.

Tables II, III and IV contain the results of the underwater weighing completed at the Olympic Training Center on many of our best men and women cyclists (2, 3). Height was recorded in centimeters (1 inch = 2.54 centimeters) and body weight in kilograms (2.2 pounds = 1 kilogram).

From the Squaw Valley results the following conclusions have been drawn as to a recommended percentage of body fat for competitive cyclists: Seniors, 6-9%; Juniors, 10-12%; Women, 12-15%. Note that these are *recommended* figures and are dependent upon the event, the time of season and body build. Research completed by Tipton and Tcheng (4, 5), however, states that the highly trained athlete should not lower his body fat below 5%. A certain amount is needed by the body for fuel, vitamin storage and insulation.

An athlete can have an evaluation of body composition done at some universities, fitness centers and YMCAs. This testing should ideally be done several times during the season. Results

TABLE I
JUNIOR MEN (March '77)

Name	Event	Height (cm)	Weight (kg)	Body Density	Percent Body Fat	LBW (kg)
G.A.	R	172	68.0	1.075	II.0	60.7
B.D.	T	178	76.6	1.083	7.9	70.5
R.R.	T	179	68.0	1.089	5.4	64.2
D.SH.	R	171	67.5	1.059	17.1	55.2
C.S.	T	177	76.6	1.070	12.9	66.7
D.SM.	R	176	66.6	1.068	13.6	58.3
P.S.	R	168	60.7	1.079	9.0	55.2
M.W.	T	188	85.9	1.065	14.7	73.3
A.W.	T & R	184	71.4	1.087	8.6	65.2
Mean		177	71.30	1.074	11.13	63.3

TABLE III
JUNIOR MEN (August '77)

Name	Event	Height	Weight	Body Density	Percent	LBW
J.B.	R	180	61.45	1.077	10.14	55.22
I.J.	R	177	63.94	1.075	10.74	57.07
M.B.	R & T	176	66.89	1.066	14.35	57.29
G.L	R	174	60.10	1.071	12.49	52.59
O:B.	T	175	68.70	1.096	2.83	55.24
Mean		176.4	64.2	1.077	10.11	55.55

TABLE IV
SENIOR WOMEN (August '77)

Name	Event	Height	Weight	Body Density	Percent	LBW
C.P.	R & T	183	72.02	1.060	15.610	60.77
B.H.	R & T	163	61.00	1.069	13.410	52.81
C.C.	R & T	183	65.31	1.066	14.615	55.76
L.L.	R & T	164	69.84	1.053	19.769	56.03
H.H.	R	162	47.61	1.076	10.717	42.51
K.R.	T	162	55.10	1.076	10.35	49.39
J.D.	T	157	58.95	1.045	23.19	45.27
Mean		167.7	61.40	1.064	15.38	51.79

are useful in making sound decisions regarding need for weight loss or gain, diet, and in establishing personal training programs.

This article and the tables were prepared in cooperation with Fredrick C. Hagerman, Gene R. Hagerman, Donald R. Kirkendall and Scott H. Nagell, who helped conduct testing on cyclists at the sports physiology laboratory at Squaw Valley. Additionally, H. R. Perez assisted with the testing of the Juniors in March at Florida State University.

References

1. Hagerman, F. C. and G. R. "Weight loss in the non-obese athlete," *Oarsman*, (March 1977), pp. 24-9.

2. Wilmore, Jack H. "The use of actual, predicted and constant residual

TABLE II
SENIOR MEN (August '77)

Name	Event	Height (cm)	Weight (kg)	Body Density	Percent Body Fat	LBW (kg)
B.W.	R	186	82.19	1.080	8.33	75.35
E.A.	R	193	80.27	1.073	11.58	70.97
S.H.	R	182	78.23	1.088	4.63	73.59
R.C.	R	168	53.15	1.079	9.41	48.15
M.P.	R	178	61.68	1.080	7.10	57.27
P.D.	R & T	184	76.19	1.080	6.79	71.02
B.C.	R	185	64.40	1.074	8.11	59.17
D.W.	R	179	65.65	1.085	7.09	60.99
L.N.	T	180	68.48	1.090	4.62	65.31
K.L.	R & T	179	64.85	1.094	3.64	62.49
L.S.	R	183	68.93	1.077	9.84	62.15
R.M.	R	178	64.96	1.074	11.39	57.56
D.G.	T	183	78.91	1.087	6.03	74.15
J.S.	T	191	85.71	1.081	8.52	78.40
G.H.	R	185	76.40	1.091	4.66	72.84
D.S.	R	179	65.76	1.080	8.84	59.95
T.P.	R	178	63.49	1.068	13.53	54.90
C.T.	R	175	71.66	1.080	8.79	65.36
F.M.	T	170	64.85	1.093	3.95	62.29
P.J.	T	180	73.02	1.049	21.32	57.45
D.P.	R	172	62.59	1.085	7.17	58.10
B.R.	R	178	67.12	1.075	10.93	59.78
L.M.	R	188	66.33	1.097	2.27	64.83
R.B.	R	182	74.00	1.081	8.69	67.57
K.M.	T	188	87.53	1.078	9.76	78.98
K.V.	R	175	63.04	1.070	12.37	55.24
Mean		166.8	70.36	1.080	8.43	64.38

volumes in the assessment of body composition by underwater weighing," *Med. Sci. Sports.*

3. Wilmore, Jack H. "A simplified method for determination of residual lung volumes," *J. Appl. Physiol.*, No. 27 (1969), pp. 96-100.

4. Tipton, C. M. and T. K. Tcheng, "Iowa wrestling study: weight loss in high school students," *JAMA, No. 214 (1970), pp. 1269-74.*

5. Tcheng, T. K. and C. M. Tipton. "Iowa wrestling study: anthropometric measurements and the prediction of a minimal weight for high school wrestlers," *Med. Sci. Sports*, No. 5 (1973), pp. 1-10.

Drill out excess fat, not components

By ED BURKE

How often have we seen riders with drilled out components, titanium frames and light wheels who, at the same time, are at least 10 pounds overweight? Why spend all the money to lighten a bike and then defeat the purpose by carrying extra weight? This article will give some insight into the benefits of weight loss, ways to lose weight, and energy expenditure at different cycling speeds.

Ten pounds may not seem like a lot of excess weight, but think about how often in cycling it must be lifted and accelerated. We have to climb hills, kick to high speed in sprints, get moving at the start and turnarounds in time trials. And extra pounds isn't the only factor — fat is composed of cells and needs a blood supply. Blood used in these cells could do more good in working muscles and in dissipating heat.

Energy to pedal the bicycle comes from the food and oxygen we consume. Food is digested in the stomach and intestine, then absorbed through the intestinal wall where it is combined with oxygen and carried to the working muscles. In a complicated process, the food and oxygen are broken down to supply energy (ATP) and carbon dioxide and water.

When energy is expended, heat is released from the working muscles. This heat production is measured in calories, a unit of heat used to express the energy value of food or the energy expenditure in work.

The scientific definition for calorie (kcal) is the amount of heat required to raise one kilogram (2.2 lbs.) of water one degree Centigrade. For example, a McDonald's Quarter Pounder with cheese contains 414 kcal, or the energy to **raise about 414 kilograms of water one degree Centigrade. The energy value of** food is measured directly by determining the amount of heat released from food when it is burned in a device called a calorimeter.

Experiments have shown that energy produced by the body's metabolism of food is equal to the heat produced by the body. For example, if you were to ride a bicycle on rollers inside a calorimeter, the change in its water temperature could be measured and your energy output calculated. The use of a calorimeter is the *direct* method of measuring energy. This is true because heat production, a specific form of energy, is being determined (1).

Scientists use oxygen consumption as an *indirect* method of measuring energy production. The amount of oxygen consumed while cycling (indirect method), when expressed in heat equivalents, will be equal to the heat produced by the body (direct method, using calorimetry). We assume that every liter of oxygen consumed equals about five kcal.

In order to keep a constant body weight, energy input has to equal energy output. If in the course of daily activity 5,000 kcal is expended, you need to eat 5,000 kcal worth of food to maintain a stable weight. Once you begin to consume extra calories, your body begins to put on extra pounds. In cycling, extra body weight means extra work to arrive at the finish line. The energy needed to carry excess bulk could otherwise be used for a breakaway effort or the final sprint.

Energy Expenditure

Just what is the energy expenditure while riding at different speeds? Assuming that the average road racing cyclist weighs 170 pounds with bicycle, oxygen consumption and metabolic heat realtionships are seen in Table 1. A caloric value of five kcal per liter of oxygen has been assumed (2). (The values are for a rider on the open road, not riding in the pack.)

Figure 1 also depicts the energy expenditure of the racing cyclist at different speeds (2). A cyclist weighing over 170 pounds or who is less efficient will move the curve upward, and a rider weighing less than 170 pounds will move the curve down.

For example, in a four and one-half hour road race in which the speed averages 23.5mph, a 170 pound cyclist will use approximately 3,500 to 4,000 kcal. Add to this the extra 1,500 kcal a day to maintain normal everyday activities and you will have to eat 5,000 to 5,5000 kcal to maintain normal body weight.

Losing Weight

The remainder of the article is for those who are interested in losing weight and becoming more efficient cyclists.

A rider can accurately find out how much body fat he or she has through body composition testing. This can be done by underwater weighing or by using skin calipers. Getting weighed on the scales cannot tell you how much of your weight is lean body weight (LBW),

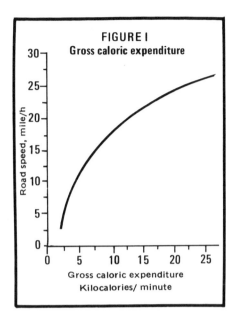

FIGURE I
Gross caloric expenditure

as opposed to fat, until your personal LBW has been determined in the lab.

Critical to weight reduction, then, is knowing how much weight can be lost safely. Once below the ideal weight (which does contain a minimum amount of fat for fuel, insulation, protection, etc.), the body begins to use protein as an alternate fuel source. Since muscle constitutes 40% of body weight and contains protein, it becomes an ideal fuel, though not one that will foster good results.

Only three methods are available for losing weight: 1) increased energy expenditure and constant food intake; 2) decreased food intake and constant

TABLE I

SPEED, POWER, AND ENERGY RELATIONSHIPS

SPEED (MPH)	HORSE POWER	OXYGEN CONSUMPTION LITERS/ MINUTE	METABOLIC HEAT (KCAL/ MINUTE)
27	0.5	4.8	24.0
25	0.4	3.9	19.5
22	0.3	3.0	15.0
19	0.2	2.1	10.5

energy expenditure; 3) a combination of 1 and 2. The first method can be accomplished by exercise programs, the second by diet.

We can all see the benefits of cutting back in our diet as a means of reducing caloric intake, but for a long time exercise has been scoffed at as a means of controlling weight. The accepted figure for melting off a pound of fat is 3,500 kcal. If you were to burn 2,000 calories a day training it would take about two days to lose a pound, according to the above figures. This, of course, is assuming you eat only enough food to maintain your other everyday activities. The problem here is that the level of training will be hard to maintain on just 1,500 kcal a day.

A long-range solution is to cut back 500 calories a day through a combination of decreased food intake and increased exercise. In a week, one pound of fat will be lost. For a cyclist who wants to lose weight rapidly, this process seems to be too slow. However, experience has shown that body weight lost gradually and systematically is more likely to stay off.

Common Misconceptions

Misconceptions about the relationship between exercise and weight control are quite common. Here are a couple of them.

Exercise and appetite—How often have you heard that the more you exercise the more you will eat? Dr. Jean Mayer (a leading nutritionist) has investigated this and concludes that daily exercise does not increase your appetite for food.

Weight reduction by sweating — Exercising with extra clothes and trying to sweat weight off will only cause temporary weight reduction. This loss has nothing to do with body fat and will not be permanent. In fact, excessive water loss can be dangerous and useless in weight control. Water does not contain calories, and fat is lost only by burning calories — not by losing water (3).

Spot reducing — There are a lot of gadgets on the market that claim to reduce fat in troublesome areas. Scientific evidence today does not support the theory that if you exercise a particular area of your body, excess fat from that region will be reduced significantly. It has been shown, though, that regular exercise which is vigorous and continuous **tends to reduce fat uniformly from all over the body.**

References

1. Katch, F. and W. McArdle. *Nutrition, Weight Control, and Exercise.* Boston: Houghton Mifflin Co., 1977.

2. Whitte, F. R. "A note on the estimation of energy expenditure of sporting cyclists," *Ergonomics,* No. 14 (1971), pp. 419-24.

3. Getchell, B. *Physical Fitness, a Way of Life.* New York: John Wiley & Sons, 1976.

Summer is wrong time for dieting and fasting

By H. R. PEREZ

The cyclists are arranged in waves at the start of the race... looking down the rows of riders you see jittery fingers tapping impatiently on handlebars... the front wheel of every bicycle in the first row edges up to the starting line....

These things are common at races, but all else is different: different styles of gloves, shorts, jerseys and helmets, sporting all the colors of the rainbow. And yet, are these the *only* differences between the competitors? Certainly not!

Every racer in the pack is different both in body structure and appearance. Indeed, even though athletes comprise a special, small segment of the population, those representing the same sport often differ as markedly as those of contrasting sports. This is true for cyclists.

Some racers are tall and some are short, but they must be highly motivated and keenly competitive if they want to win. And it is the quest for victory that often causes cyclists to consider losing weight in order to improve performance.

Common Misconception

A common misconception often taken for truth is that if the body is lighter in weight it can go faster. This is true if all other things are equal; that is, if other physical qualities remain the same. Unfortunately, this won't always be the case after weight loss. Frequently strength, a very important determinant of athletic success, is unintentionally lost along with weight. The purpose of this article is to put you on guard concerning weight loss as the hot summer months approach.

With the arrival of the racing season, you should be carefully monitoring your weight and body composition. Much of the racing that lies ahead is going to be under hot and humid conditions, and body weight can't help but fluctuate to some degree. But a cyclist who decides to diet or fast to intentionally lower body weight (and presumably become more competitive) may instead be inviting less than winning performance.

A loss in physical efficiency may result from an inadequate diet. It is dangerous to knowingly or accidentally restrict nutrient intake during hot weather when metabolism (internal chemical reactions brought on by nutrient breakdown) is already elevated due to the heat. During the summer racing season a balanced diet is necessary to ensure that your body's tissues are getting the adequate amounts of nutrients necessary for maintaining a high level of physical activity. A considerable set-back may result if you try to manipulate your body weight after entering this time of year.

Lose Weight, Lose Strength

One of the major problems that weight loss can bring on is a loss of strength. There's no disputing that strength correlates well with athletic performance. A cyclist who loses weight in order to ride faster can instead become physically weaker from inadequate protein intake and/or retention. Thus, the reason for which dieting was undertaken—gain in speed—is negated by the result—loss of strength.

Dieting during the summer months can be dangerous in other respects. Not only will energy be lacking for workouts and races, but fluids and nutrient sources escape from the body more quickly. Water is stored in carbohydrates (sugars and starches), which are utilized first in energy production. When depleted of such stores there is initial weight loss. Then, as carbohydrates are exhausted in the liver and muscles where they are stored, fats and proteins become larger providers of body energy. This is what causes pounds to be shed.

It must be remembered that proteins contain nitrogen, whereas fats and carbohydrates do not. Only proteins can provide the essential materials for muscular growth, maintenance and repair. A reduction in voluntary protein intake (through diet) or a loss in protein due to its breakdown for energy will result in a significant strength reduction. Certainly a loss in weight is not worth the sacrifice in terms of strength. Since muscular strength is so important to cycling performance, precautions need to be taken to safeguard it.

Proper Protein Ratio

During the summer racing season, a well-balanced diet should be followed. In addition to vitamins, minerals, fats and carbohydrates, adequate levels of protein should be ingested. For most cyclists, one gram of protein for every kilogram (2.2 pounds) of body weight is recommended each day. This amounts to about 10-15% of all the calories ingested. A larger intake is not advised since most cyclists consume more calories at each meal than inactive individuals, thus ensuring adequate protein for body size and weight.

In conclusion, since the summer's heat and humidity will take its heavy toll on the physiology of the body, it is not prudent to impose an additional burden such as dieting and fasting. Caloric restriction should be left for the fall and winter when racing tails off and small losses in strength are not so important.

Ergogenic aids no substitute for proper training

By ED BURKE

"The merciless rigor of modern competitive sports, especially at the international level, the glory of victory, and the growing social and economic reward of sporting success (in no way any longer related to reality) increasingly forces athletes to improve their performance by any means available." So states the 1972 *Manual on Doping*, published by the Medical Commission of the International Olympic Committee. Several recent events illustrate the problem:

—Suggestions that "steroids" were used by several cyclists at the 1978 World Championships. Three athletes were found positive; they were not disqualified because the UCI decided that there had been errors in the way the test routine was carried out.

—Statements by Bernard Thevenet that his poor performance in 1978 was due to massive doses of hormone drugs. His troubles stem from cortisone, a drug which so affected various vital organs that he became unable to compete.

—The East German pursuiter disqualified for using ephedrine, a sympathomimetic stimulant which some think will improve an athlete's performance.

Many scientists agreed that there is a chemical technology race under way in sports. Trainers, coaches and athletes are continually experimenting with various stimulants and other drugs to improve performance. These are often referred to as ergogenic aids (3).

Four of these which have made the headlines recently will be reviewed in this article.

Ephedrine

Let us first look at ephedrine, an ingredient contained in countless prescription and over-the-counter medications used to treat respiratory ailments. It is on the IOC banned list because some think that as a sympathomimetic it will stimulate athletic performance (4).

Ephedrine is believed to affect the sympathetic nervous system, which is a division of the autonomic nervous system. The ANS controls many functions of the body that are not normally controlled voluntarily, such as glandular secretions and heart rate. The sympathetic nervous system is concerned with energy expenditure, increasing the heart rate and cardiac output, and the release of adrenaline (which also increases energy output).

No favorable effect has been demonstrated using ephedrine in athletics. But because both ephedrine and pseudoephedrine are widely distributed and used in either oral or spray form, a cyclist who innocently takes a cold medication could end up disqualified. The danger lies in the way tests are now conducted, since any trace of a banned substance in the urine is considered doping. Many authorities are hoping for new regulations to make a distinction between pharmacological and ergogenic levels.

Caffeine

Until 1972, when formal testing

procedures were introduced at the Olympics, caffeine was among the list of drugs banned by the IOC. However, it has since been removed from the banned list, possibly due to the acceptance and use of coffee, a main source of caffeine, by millions of people around the world.

For many years cyclists have been drinking small quantities of strong coffee near the end of the race to receive that last "kick." The July 1978 issue of *Runner's World* (5) had a cover story about coffee and its effects on increased performance. Since the release of this article the use of caffeine has gained even more popularity.

Caffeine, chemically, is trimethylated xanthine. It is found naturally in coffee beans, tea leaves, kola nuts, cocoa and mate (6). The table shows the approximate amount of caffeine in various sources. For beverages, the amounts shown are the approximate concentrations found in each cup or glass. For drugs and other preparations, this is the amount found in each tablet.

Caffeine, like amphetamine , stimulates the central nervous system. It has been found to pass across the blood-brain barrier with a quickness similar to alcohol's. It is known to alter several central nervous system neurotransmitter functions associated with body regulation. These include stimulation of all parts of the cerebral cortex, as well as respiration and circulation. Caffeine also dilates coronary arteries and increases the heart's force of contraction (6). It is no wonder with all these clinical manifestations that cyclists will use caffeine at the end of a long road race.

Acute intake of caffeine has been shown to increase performance times of athletes (5,7). Any time there can be a release of free fatty acids to provide energy for work, carbohydrates can be spared. Caffeine has the ability to do this, producing an increase in the burning of fat for energy.

After reading this you might want to start taking coffee or caffeine tablets before and during your races. But don't do it before knowing some of the hazards involved. Tea and coffee are also diuretics; that is, they stimulate the flow of urine. This may cause discomfort during the event, and it could compound the serious problem of fluid loss in hot weather.

Many stomachs are sensitive to large doses of caffeine, resulting in internal disturbance during the race. Those who habitually drink coffee will less likely be affected by its side effects, but less aided by the caffeine stimulation. So think twice before you guzzle that second or third cup before the race.

Anabolic Steroids

Although they have been banned internationally, steroids, which are taken in tablets and through injection, have remained a source of controversy. They are used on the theory that they will help an athlete become stronger and faster.

Anabolic steroids refer to those drugs that mimic testosterone, the male hormone which increases muscle mass. With this in mind it is obvious why sprinters and kilometer riders would want to use steroids, but why the news that road riders are now turning to them? It is because they stimulate red blood cell formation, which adds to the capacity of blood to carry oxygen. Testosterone has also been shown to enhance the levels of glycogen in the muscles, a condition which is related to resistance to fatigue (8).

There are very few adverse effects to normal doses of anabolic steroids when administered under a physician's supervision. Athletes, however, are using massive doses under the assumption that if a little is good, a lot is better. But this has been leading to gastrointestinal disturbances, liver disfunction, jaundice, increase in blood pressure and acne. Prostatic troubles can occur, as can testicular shrinkage and a decrease in spermatogenesis. In females, masculinization symptoms and menstrual troubles are possible.

Another danger is an increase in tendon strength out of proportion with muscular strength. Inflammation and rupture of the tendons may occur. Also, bones are subjected to increased stress and permanent lesions will appear (9). For these reasons an athlete who takes steroids is chancing permanent medical complications. This should be sufficient warning against them.

Cortisone

Cortisol is a hormone produced by the body. It is essential to most, if not

**AMOUNTS OF CAFFEINE
IN VARIOUS PRODUCTS**

Beverages	Mg caffeine
Brewed coffee	100-150/cup
Instant coffee	.86-99/cup
Tea	.60-75/cup
Decaffeinated coffee	2-4/cup
Cola drinks	40-60/glass

Stimulants	
No-Doz	100/tablet
Vivarine	200/tablet

Cold preparations	
Over-the-counter	30/tablet

Analgesics	
Anacin, Cope, Midol	32/tablet
Vanquish	60/tablet
Excedrin	66/tablet

all, body functions, especially carbohydrate, protein and fat metabolism. Cortisone is a commercial name for cortisol, along with brands such as Prednisolone and Triamcinoline. These drugs reduce redness, swelling and tenderness resulting from sprains and strains.

Adverse reactions to cortisone are related to dose and time; the longer the duration of use and the higher the dosage, the greater the incidence of adverse effects. Single doses are devoid of risk. Chronic administration can lead to a swollen face, glucose intolerance, increased susceptibility to infection, peptic ulcers, mental changes, fluid retention, hypertension, acne and cataracts (10).

Is it any wonder why cyclists who use anabolic steroids and cortisone have such short careers?

Blood Doping

Did he or didn't he? That was the question asked of Finland's Lasse Viren, the 5,000 and 10,000 meter track champion, at the 1976 Olympics. Was he using the technique of blood doping to increase performance?

Here's how it works: 500-1,000ml of blood are withdrawn from the athlete three to four weeks prior to competition. The athlete continues to train, and with the help of exercise and diet the blood which has been removed will be regenerated. Then, just before competition, the athlete is reinfused with his own blood. In theory this helps improve performance due to an overabundance of red blood cells to carry oxygen. After the gold medals of Lasse Viren, the incidence of blood doping is said to have increased among international athletes attempting to improve their endurance.

Until recently, research has concluded that blood doping may not improve performance. This is because an increased red blood cell count increases the blood's viscosity, which in turn reduces the heart's ability to pump blood to the muscles (11). Also, an athlete's muscles may not be able to use the additional oxygen, a factor controlled by aerobic enzyme levels. And there were some technical problems in the storing of blood until Gledhill (12) recently developed the glycerol freezing technique, which allows reinfusion to be delayed indefinitely. Upon reinfusion, he found that blood RBC, hemoglobin and hematocrit values increased 8% after 24 hours and 11% after one week before gradually returning to normal levels.

Buick et al (13) used a double-blind study to show that after reinfusion of blood into highly trained endurance runners hemoglobin increased 8% and oxygen consumption by 4 ml/kg. They concluded that blood doping increases maximum VO_2 and extends endurance in highly trained runners. Advantages last up to one week, they said.

Williams et al (14) investigated the effects of blood infusion upon the endurance capacity in 16 long distance runners, 13 of whom were marathoners. They were tested before blood withdrawal, two hours after reinfusion and then again a week later. The athletes ran to exhaustion on a treadmill each time. The results showed no significant differences in performance, even though hemoglobin counts had increased.

Although some investigators and athletes may contend that blood doping can improve performance, the available literature does not provide physiological rationale or sufficient objective evidence to back them up (15). Blood doping can be dangerous and, in my opinion, should not be condoned by coaches or physicians.

During the 1976 Summer Olympics more than 2,000 dope tests were performed. Eleven positive results were reported, eight of which were for anabolic steroids. Therefore, only three cases involved the use of regularly banned drugs, the lowest incidence at the Olympics since testing was begun (16). Further research and refinements in laboratory procedures will better control the use of anabolic steroids.

While improving performance with the use of ergogenic aids and drugs may be possible, danger is present. The cyclist and coach will do much better to concentrate on proper conditioning and dedicated training.

References

1. Prohop, L. *The Problem of Doping.* Lausanne, Switz: International Olympic Medical Publication, 1972.

2. Percy, E. "Ergogenic aids in athletics," *Med. Sci. Sports,* No. 10 (1978), pp. 298-303.

3. Morgan, W., ed. *Ergogenic Aids and Muscular Performance.* Academic Press, 1972.

4. Bender, K., *et. al.* "Use of medications by U.S. Olympic swimmers," *Physician and Sports Med.,* (Nov. 1977), pp. 63-5.

5. "Coffee makes longer easier," *Runner's World,* (July 1978), pp. 52-3.

6. Greden, J. "Coffee, tea and you," *The Sciences,* (Jan. 1979), pp. 6-11.

7. Costill, D. "Effects of caffeine ingestion on metabolism and exercise performance," *Med. Sci. Sports,* No. 10 (1978), pp. 155-8.

8. Edington, D. and V. Edgerton. *The Biology of Physical Activity.* Boston: Houghton Mifflin Co., 1976.

9. Dirix, A. "Anabolic steroids and sport." Montreal: IOC Medical Controls, 1976.

10. Bochner, F., *et. al. Handbook of Clinical Pharmacology.* Boston: Little, Brown and Co., 1978.

11. Replogle, R. and E. Merrill. "Experimental polycythemia and hemodilution," *J. of Thorasic Cardiovascular Surgery,* No. 60 (1970), pp. 582-8.

12. Gledhill, N., *et. al.* "An optimal method of storing blood for blood boosting," *Med. Sci. Sports,* No. 19 (1978), p. 40.

13. Buick, F., *et. al.* "Double blind study of blood boosting in highly trained runners," *Med. Sci. Sports,* No. 10 (1978) p. 49.

14. Williams, M., *et. al.* "The effect of blood infusion upon endurance capacity and rating of perceived exertion," *Med. Sci. Sports,* No. 10 (1978), pp. 113-8.

15. Williams, M. "Blood doping—does it really help athletes?" *Phys. and Sports Med.,* (Jan. 1975), pp. 52-6.

16. Laurin, C., *et. al.* "Medical report of the Montreal olympic games," *Am. J. Sports Med.,* No. 6 (1978), pp. 54-61.

Don't be a dope — know what's in medicine

By ED BURKE
and KATERI DAMES

Ever since the early six-day races, cyclists have sought the magic ingredient that would give them the mental and physical strength to complete and win such grueling events. The use of drugs and other substances to improve maximal performance is as old as athletic competition itself.

Exactly what constitutes "doping" is a matter of considerable debate. Clearly, drug use in sports is not synonymous with drug misuse. Many athletes receive prescribed drugs for specific ailments. But a problem arises when the medica-

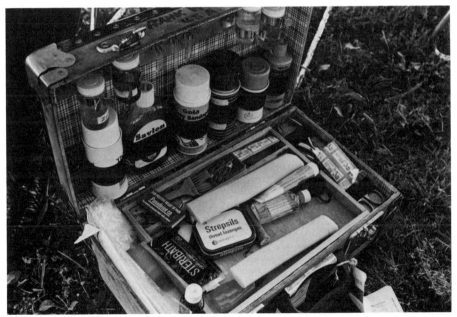

A trainer or coach for a cycling team will often pack an assortment of medications. With such a kit he will be able to treat all kinds of aches, pains and even digestive problems. But it is essential that trainers and racing cyclists be aware of and avoid any medication containing substances that have been ruled as illegal aids to performance by the sports' governing body, the UCI.

tion contains chemicals which also are able to improve the athlete's performance.

As an example, in the 1972 Olympics swimmer Rich Demont had his medal recalled after he won the 400 meter freestyle. Apparently he had not stopped taking a pharmaceutical product he'd used to ease his asthmatic breathing, and his urine sample was found to contain two substances banned from the Olympics.

Literature on cycling tells of many doping incidents, some which even led to death. During the 1960 Olympics a cyclist collapsed after using a vasodilating drug which along with heat stress probably caused an overburdening of his heart. A pro cyclist, Tom Simpson, died on a steep climb during the 1967 Tour de France and was found to have taken amphetamine (speed).

Drug use in sports is of great concern and has been the subject of much discussion. Many athletic governing bodies have rules which state that whether done unknowingly, secretly or openly, the use of performance improving drugs is condemned.

The medical commission of the International Olympic Committee defines doping as "the administration of or the use by a competing athlete of any substance foreign to the body or of any physiological substance taken in abnormal quantity or taken by an abnormal route of entry into the body, with the sole intention of increasing in an artificial and unfair manner his performance in competition."

Specific drugs forbidden by the IOC Medical Advisory Committee are:

Psychomotor Stimulant Drugs: amphetamine, benzphetamine, cocaine, dicthylpropion, dimethylamphetamine, ethylamphetamine, fencamfamin, fenproporex, methylamphetamine, mechylphenidate, norpseudoephedrine, pemoline, phendimetrazine, phenmetrazine, phentermine, pipradol, prolintane, and related compounds.

Sympathomimetic Amines: ephedrine, methoxyphenamine, methylephedrine, and related compounds.

Narcotic Analgesics: morphine, heroin, methadone, pethidine, dextromoramide, dipipanone, and related compounds.

Other Central Nervous System Stimulants: amphenzole, bemegride, leptazole, nihethamide, strychnine, and related compounds.

Anabolic Steroids: methandienone (Dianabol, Danabol), ethyloestrenol (Maxibolin, Orabolin), methandriol (Stenediol), stanozolol (Winstrol, Stombh), nadrolone phenpropionate (Durabolin), and related compounds.

The list of prohibited products drawn up by the medical board and ratified by the director of the UCI are:

Amphetamine, dimethylamphetamine, ethylamphetamine, norfenfluramine, furfurylmethylamphetamine, phentermine, clorphentermine, cyclopentamine, pipradol, phenmetrazine, diethylpropion, fencamine, permoline, strychnine, ephedrine and pseudo ephedrine, heptaminol, bemegride, nikethamide, mephentermine, aletamine, methylphenidate, phacetoperane, phendimetrazine, prolintane, tranylcypramine, cypenamine, ibogaine, aminophenazone, leptazol, anabolic steroids, and related compounds.

Some common substances taken by athletes which will show positive in doping tests are: Visine Eye Drops, Vicks Nasal Spray, Neo-Synephrine Drops, Vicks Throat Lozenges, Actifed, Coricidin-D, Brokotabs, Demazin, Brondilate, Iso-Tabs 60, Triaminicin.

Athletes should avoid these problem medications altogether or at least discontinue their use for 48 to 72 hours before the event to ensure a negative urine sample. If unable to do this at the time of competition, consult a physician to see if there is a similar substance that is not on the banned list.

As more U.S. cyclists begin to enter international competition they may unwittingly rather than intentionally use medications which will lead to disqualification. The UCI rule book calls for a one-month suspension for the first offense of an amateur; three months for the second offense; and confiscation of the license for the third offense. To avoid this predicament all cyclists and their physicians, coaches and trainers should become familiar with this information on pharmacological agents and the regulations regarding their use in competition.

Reference
1. Williams, M. *Drugs and Athletic Performance.* Springfield, IL: Charles C. Thomas, 1974.

Injuries

Beware of wind chill during early season rides

By ED BURKE

During February and March northern cyclists must think about riding in cold weather. Many prefer to sit on the rollers in the warmth of their homes, but as the racing season nears it's hard to resist venturing outside, even when the mercury hovers around zero.

The first consideration should be when to ride, and the wind-chill index is probably the best guide. The adjoining chart provides factors to consider when going out in the windy cold. The cyclist who faces temperatures in the areas labeled "Great Danger" is only asking for trouble. "Increasing Danger" signals that special care should be used in dressing. "Little Danger" signifies just that.

Direction of the wind can also be a crucial factor. A side or tail wind has but a fraction of the impact of a head wind. And, of course, the faster you ride into the wind the more the wind-chill is increased. It may be wise to begin your workout into the wind so that the second half will find it at your back. In this way perspiration will not be as dangerous or as uncomfortable when skin temperature begins to drop.

To judge wind speed, look at the trees. At 20mph, small branches move and dust or snow is raised; at 30, large branches move; at 40, whole trees move. You can just feel a 10 mph wind lightly on your face.

On very cold days you may consider breaking up the workout into two parts,

Wind-chill Chart

AIR TEMPERATURE (Degrees Farenheit)								
Wind Speed (M.P.H.)	Adapted from: ENCYCLOPEDIA OF ATHLETIC MEDICINE							
	+50	+40	+30	+20	+10	0	-10	-20
5	48	37	27	16	6	-5	-15	-26
10	40	28	16	4	-9	-24	-33	-46
15	36	22	9	-5	-18	-32	-45	-58
20	32	18	4	-10	-25	-39	-53	-67
25	30	16	0	-15	-29	-44	-59	-74
30	28	13	-2	-18	-33	-48	-63	-79
35	27	11	-4	-20	-35	-51	-67	-82
40	26	10	-6	-21	-37	-53	-69	-85
	LITTLE DANGER				INCREASING DANGER			GREAT DANGER

When beginning to train for the new season, a big problem is cold temperatures. Further, even on calm days a cyclist moving at 15-20 miles per hour creates a wind-chill temperature far below what the thermometer reads.

going out once in the morning and again in the afternoon.

Clothing

Cold weather clothing should protect all the skin surface. The effectiveness of the insulation depends on the layers of clothing and how well they trap the air; it is more sensible to wear several layers than to put on a T-shirt and a heavy jacket. Remember that the wind-chill chart has two variables (temperature and wind) and one should dress accordingly. When the temperature is 10 below with very little wind, dress for the cold. But when it is 10 above with a 20mph breeze, make sure you wear something which will help keep the wind out.

Never ride without a hat. The head is one part of your anatomy which loses heat rapidly in cold weather. A pull-over mask can be added when needed. Mittens will keep hands warmer than gloves because they merge the heat of the hand and each finger. Feet can be kept warmer by wearing one pair of socks, slipping into plastic baggies, and then adding another pair of socks. Plastic toe clip covers also help block the wind.

If the weather is likely to change for the worse or if roads are in poor condition, it is a wise idea to ride a pre-determined route that is known by someone at home. Riding with another person is also sensible, in case of emergency.

How often has someone tried to dissuade you from exercising in the cold by saying you will freeze your lungs? Documented literature to substantiate this concern is virtually non-existent.

One problem which can occur, however, is frostbite. When the temperature is below freezing the hands, ears, nose, fingers and toes can be in danger. Frostbite should not be thought of lightly since it can disable or kill. If you ever suspect frostbite, do not walk on or massage the frozen parts. Place them in water that is about body temperature and seek medical help as soon as possible.

By following these precautionary measures, you will be able to put in those 2,000 road miles before the spring with more safety and comfort.

References

1. Davies, George. "Running with the winter cold," *Cardio-Gram*, 3, No. 6 (1977).

2. Sheehan, George. "Compensating for cold," *Encyclopedia of Athletic Medicine*. Mt. View, CA: World Publications, 1972.

R$_x$ for saddle sores and road rash

By ED BURKE

When you are in the racing season it's important not to lose valuable riding time due to injuries or sickness. Three problems which are both frequent and disabling are saddle sores, road rash, and sore leg muscles.

That part of your anatomy on which everything in cycling "hinges," the groin area, needs to have friction kept to a minimum. In this part of the body, cleanliness cannot be stressed too often as a help in preventing saddle soreness and avoiding saddle boils.

Boils usually occur from irritation to hair follicles. The predominant bacterial infection (staphylococcus) produces a pustule. The pustule becomes enlarged, reddened, and hard from internal pressure. As pressure increases, extreme pain and tenderness develop.

Most boils will mature and rupture, emitting their contents. Boils should *not* be squeezed, since squeezing forces the infection into adjacent tissue or other skin areas. Avoid irritation and bring boils to maturity by means of hot compresses or by antibacterial ointment.

As with most skin infections, scrupulous attention to body hygiene may prevent many problems. Shorts and chamois should be washed (using mild soap) after every use to remove chamois lubricant, sweat, grit, etc. Cleaning the groin with rubbing alcohol will serve as an antiseptic and it will toughen the skin.

There are various lubricants that will keep the chamois of your riding shorts soft and clean. Store-bought products such as Noxzema and Kucharik's Chamois Fat are excellent for this purpose. Frank Westell, trainer for 1976 Olympic teams, had his own formula of Vaseline, lanolin, cod liver oil, and vitamin E.

Road Rash

Road rash is an abrasion, and if you haven't "caught" any you're bound to before long. Simply, it's when the skin is worn away due to scraping against a rough surface, exposing numerous blood vessels. This general exposure, with dirt and foreign material penetrating the skin, increases the probability that infection will result unless the wound is properly cleaned.

Clean the area with soap and water and get out the grit with a brush. Apply a solution of hydrogen peroxide over abraded area and continue until foaming has subsided. Apply a petroleum-base medicated ointment (Neosporin ointment) to keep the abraded surface moist. In cycling, it is not desirable for abrasions to acquire a scab.

Place a non-adhering sterile pad (Telfa pad) over the ointment. Change the dressing daily and look for signs of infection. If you haven't had a tetanus shot in a few years, you should get a tetanus antitoxin no later than 24 hours after the injury.

Infection becomes apparent within two to seven days, with the wound becoming red, swollen, hot and tender. Lymph glands near the infection (groin, arm) become swollen and painful, and there may be a fever. A physician should be consulted to stave off further complications.

Some precautions may be followed to keep road rash troubles to a minimum. Wear a light cotton shirt under your jersey. In the event of a fall, this will allow the jersey to slide over the shirt and your abrasions may not be as widespread. Shaving your legs will help to minimize the amount of skin lost and aid in the healing process. You will find cleaning and bandaging the wound is easier without hair present.

Keeping Out Cold

During early season racing and training, remember that it is safer to be too warm than too cold. A large piece of thin plastic under the jersey front and back can be used to keep out cold wind and rain, and it can be easily removed if you get overheated.

When your legs are bare they should be kept warm enough for maximum efficiency and protection from strain. Vaseline or something similar can be used to coat the knees; warm analgesic balm may be more helpful on very cold days. Some *soigneurs* prefer to use a rubbing oil before the race which contains capsicum or wintergreen to add a little heat.

In training, I can see no point in riding without leg warmers if the temperature is below 65F degrees. In cycling, remember, you always have the addition of wind chill in cooling the skin.

After a hard training ride or race, you should immediately clean your body with rubbing alcohol and change into warm, dry clothing. Better still, take a shower. Try to remain in a warm place until recovered.

During hot weather there's no need to apply ointments to your legs. This is the time when you can enjoy the cooling effect of air over skin.

Cleanliness is the key to curing and preventing saddle sores. Wash shorts after every ride and if possible hang them outside to dry — the ultraviolet rays in sunlight will help kill bacteria. The lineup above is part of the collection of John Allis, former national team rider.

Ice your leg injuries for fast healing

By ED BURKE

Of all the injuries in cycling the most prevalent are to the muscle-tendon-ligament complex of the legs. This article will present an overview of these soft-tissue injuries and explain the use of cold and heat in rehabilitation.

These injuries can be classified as direct and indirect. Direct injuries, which are usually the result of an accident, can be further divided into levels of severity. Indirect injuries are the result of repetitive overuse of the tissue complex or injury to the structures associated with muscle function (bursa, tendon sheath, etc.).

Direct Injuries

Muscle contusions of the leg usually are caused by a fall. The usual mechanism of the injury is that the muscle and associated tissue are crushed between the pavement and the bone.

A *muscle strain* is a partial disruption of the continuity of a muscle or tendon. A tendon connects muscle to bone. When the leg muscle is contracted violently while under full stretch, or when the muscle tendon is taken past its normal range of motion, you have a strain. Once again this usually occurs in an accident.

You can help prevent injury by developing a strong and flexible muscle. Flexibility through stretching is the subject of another article in this book.

After a muscle contusion or strain, ice bags should be applied immediately and kept in position for 30 to 45 minutes. Cold therapy should be used twice daily. When the ice is removed, a light foam rubber pad should be placed over the injured area and secured with an elastic bandage wrap. The leg should be elevated. The objective is to have light compression on the area to help discourage swelling and further internal bleeding. At no time should heat be applied to an acute injury.

Pain, tenderness, swelling and range of motion vary with the severity of each contusion or strain. Discoloration of the skin (black and blue) may appear within 24 hours in severe injuries, and range of motion is usually quite limited. Mild contusions and strains are characterized by minimal pain, tenderness and swelling, but no restriction of motion.

There is no limit on the duration of ice therapy. It should be continued daily until the acute signs and symptoms subside completely and full range of motion is returned. The hard thigh mass (hematoma) will begin to soften in three to seven days. You should do flexion and extension exercises as much as can be tolerated, but no forced range of motion exercising or riding should be undertaken. In cases of severe contusions or strains, see a physician to rule out the possibility of fracture or internal injuries.

When can you return to racing? The answer is simple: You may race again when the symptoms return to a mild state and you have regained near-normal function. An elastic bandage wrap may be helpful in some instances.

A *sprain*, by definition, indicates that the continuity of a ligament has been

Leg injuries, both external and internal, are common in cycling. When the problem is with muscles and tendons, the initial treatment should be application of cold to limit swelling.

partially disrupted. A ligament connects bone to bone. All sprains should be immediately treated with the same ice procedure used for strains. Between treatments the sprained area should be protected with an elastic wrap. If a severe injury is suspected, the athlete should see a physician immediately.

Indirect Injuries

Bursitis is caused by either overuse or contusion. There are many bursae in the lower limb, 18 of which are located in the knee. These can easily become inflamed by pushing a big gear, pedaling from an incorrect position, or riding without leg warmers on a cold day. Bursae are small sacs which contain the synovial fluid that helps lubricate the joints.

General treatment for bursitis includes rest from cycling as much as possible. Ice application, because of its anti-inflammatory action, is very impor-

tant. After a few days mild heat and massage can be applied.

The three most common types of tendon strains caused by repetitive activities are patellar, Achilles and popliteal *tendinitis.*

Patellar tendinitis occurs to the tendon which connects the knee cap to the tibia (lower leg bone) and is caused by overuse of the quadriceps muscles on the front of the thigh.

Achilles tendinitis occurs in the tendon which connects the gastrocnemius (calf muscle) to the calcaneus (heel bone). It can result from improper seat height or pedal action.

Popliteal tendinitis is common in cycling, and is caused by the continuous locking and unlocking of the knee. This causes the popliteal tendon (rear and outside of knee) to rub on the ligament which connects the femur and fibula (lateral collateral ligament). This results in inflammation of the tendon, the ligament and/or the bursae between them. The usual cause is a too-high seat.

A similar treatment applies to all three tendon injuries: application of ice, rest, and local massage and heat after inflammation has subsided.

Tenosynovitis, inflammation of the synovial membrane of a tendon, is usually caused by unaccustomed overuse. The synovial membrane holds the fluids which help lubricate the joints. The two most common locations of the problem are the Achilles and peroneal tendons. The latter runs along the posterior outside the ankle.

Tenosynovitis can be caused by improper foot placement on the pedal, bio-mechanical foot defects, or poor pedaling technique. Treatment consists of rest from riding and application of ice or immersion in cold water. After inflammation has subsided, mild heat and massage can be useful. Heel lifts can then be used to limit movement of the Achilles tendon, and the peroneal tendon can be wrapped or taped for added support.

Shin splints are usually caused by sudden unaccustomed overuse of the flexor muscles located in the front of the lower leg. The irritation takes place at the origin of the sheath which connects the two bones there. Speculation about the causes includes faulty shoe alignment on the pedals, overuse stress, and arch problems with the feet.

Healing of shin splints is slow and is hindered further by the reduced blood supply to the area. Treatment consists of prolonged icing sessions of 20 to 30 minutes on the entire front and inside edge of the shinbone. Arch supports and stretching may help, as will the use of aspirin for relief of pain and inflammation.

Cold, Not Heat

There is often disagreement and confusion among coaches and cyclists about whether to apply cold or heat to an injury. The observations, experiments and experience of many in sports medicine decidedly point to the use of cold in the treatment of acute injuries to control swelling and internal bleeding.

The rationale for the use of cold (cryotherapy) is based on physiologic responses. Cold initially limits the blood flow to the area, thereby diminishing the amount of hemorrhage in the muscle, tendon or ligament.

It is reasonable to assume that the decreased temperature produces a slowing of metabolic processes within the tissue. This in turn diminishes the need for nutrients, which are carried by the blood through the capillary bed. Therefore, a reduction in metabolism results in a reduction of swelling. This is why cold is important in achieving early control of the injury.

The application of heat to an acute injury has the opposite effect. Heat increases blood flow and metabolic rate, thus fostering the inflammation and swelling.

As a general rule we can say that cold, compression and elevation should be used in the initial treatment of all acute cycling injuries.

Use massage to rub out fatigue

By ED BURKE

Massage is a variety of systematic manipulations of body tissues for therapeutic purposes. It aids the venous and lymphatic return and prevents stoppage of blood in the capillaries of the muscles.

Massage produces an increase of blood flow as well as heightened interchange of substances between the blood stream and tissue cells. Secondary effects include an increase in peripheral blood flow and a decrease in the swelling of muscle cells. Mechanical stretching can be effectively accomplished by a friction type of massage.

In general, massage is used for relief of pain, relaxation of muscle tension, improvement of circulation, reduction of edema, and stretching.

Massage will not directly increase strength of normal muscles, although as a means to an end it is more effective than rest in promoting recovery from fatigue produced by excessive cycling. It cannot be stated that massage will increase muscle tone or prevent atrophy in muscle tissue that has been injured. Claims have been made that massage will reduce fat deposits in muscles, though research has found no evidence to support this theory.

One benefit often forgotten in a discussion of massage is its psychological effect. Most cyclists enjoy the soothing effects of massage even when muscular fatigue is not that great.

The soigneur or masseur wishes to help a cyclist's muscles maintain the best possible state of health, flexibility and vitality so that after recovery from a hard ride the muscles can function at their maximum potential.

The following points are essential for good technique in athletic massage.

Rhythm

A steady rhythm is essential to help relax the cyclist. This is established by making the interval between each stroke the same. To obtain good rhythm a masseur must assume a comfortable position. This requires that the cyclist be on a table with a minimum height of 28 inches. The masseur should assume a standing position next to the table which permits the hands to move over a large area. A swaying motion with the body will help produce rhythmical strokes while avoiding unnecessary fatigue of the back.

Lubricants

All massage should be directly to the skin, using a lubricant to avoid irritation and ensure smooth contact. Cold cream or baby oil can be used, but heavy oil should be avoided so there isn't a large amount left on the skin. Some cyclists prefer a fine talcum powder, but this sometimes won't allow a satisfactory grasping of the muscle tissues.

Position

The cyclist should be lying on the table in a comfortable position, and should be kept warm. When face up, a pillow should be placed under the head and a rolled towel behind the knees. When face down, a pillow should be under the abdomen, a towel under the ankles to prevent hyper-flexion of the foot, and no pillow under the head.

The massage routine should be carried out systematically and in a quiet room. The masseur should talk about things besides the race and training since he is trying to relax the rider as much as possible. Start with light stroking, followed by deeper stroking, kneading, friction and percussion movements. At all times you should be conscious of the cyclist's response to the pressures you are applying.

Movements

In modern scientific massage the following terms are used:

STROKING (effleurage) is the manipulation toward the heart of large areas, done with varying speeds and pressures with hands molded to the body. Stroking must be very light, gently making and breaking contact with the skin. A skillful technique is necessary in order to obtain the soothing effect.

Deep stroking is used to assist the venous and lymphatic circulation. The term deep massage does not imply that great force should be used since this may irritate or injure the muscles. The pressure should be just heavy enough to stimulate flow to the nearest lymph glands, which are located at the junction of the arm and shoulder and behind the knee and groin area. All heavy pressure should be directed toward the heart.

KNEADING consists of grasping a muscle, applying and releasing pressure, then progressing to an adjacent area and repeating the process. Again, movements should be toward the heart and lymph glands. This form of manipulation stimulates the large muscles and improves circulation.

PERCUSSION movements include hacking with the border of the hand, clapping with cupped hands, tapping with the finger tips, and beating with the heel of the hand. Percussion movements should not be used on severely fatigued or injured muscles.

FRICTION movements are done with the finger tips and thumbs to aid in local circulation around joints such as knee, ankle and wrist. The superficial tissues are moved over the underlying structures in a circular motion, helping loosen ligaments and tendons around the joint.

Treatment

The cyclist should not be required to move or turn from side to side any more than necessary during the massage. The following order should be followed during the treatment:

1. Start with the rider on his back and begin with the feet, using friction movements. Concentrate on the arch under the ball of the foot and the long arch on the inside of the foot.

2. On the back of the leg begin with light stroking extending from the ankle all the way to the buttocks. Continue into deep stroking and kneading movements on the calf and hamstring muscles. Spend about five minutes on each limb.

3. Next move to the muscles of the buttock and lower back. These muscles become increasingly sore after pushing a big gear or climbing. Use stroking and kneading movements and spend about five minutes on this area.

4. If the cyclist complains of soreness in the shoulders, spend a few minutes on the upper back, neck and shoulders to loosen the muscles there.

5. Next, have the cyclist turn over. Apply light stroking from the top of the foot, over the knee and to the top of the thigh. Use friction motion on the skin area and around the knee cap. Pay particular attention to the thigh, for here lie the power muscles of pedaling. After light stroking proceed with deep stroking and kneading techniques. It is important to knead the inside, middle and outside of the thigh. Five minutes on each thigh should do it.

A complete massage after a hard race will take at least 30 minutes, and should leave the cyclist feeling physically and psychologically improved. Massage should be done in the evening, and about 60-90 minutes after the evening meal. This will allow time for the food to be partially digested so more blood can be directed to the muscles.

When Not to Massage

There are situations for which massage is not recommended and it is important that the masseur know them. Included are cases of skin infec-

Massage is a way to help loosen and warm up muscles before an event, as well as a means to aid recovery afterward.

tions, acute inflammation, skin lesions, temperature over 100F degrees, acute circulatory disorder, such as phlebitis, varicose veins and thrombosis, and muscle contusions.

The techniques of massage can be mastered only through experience. Common sense and knowledge of the procedures will help a masseur assist a rider to faster recovery, enabling muscles to soon function again at their maximum.

Recommended Reading
1. Tappan, F. M. *Massage Techniques.* New York: MacMillan Co., 1961.

2. Licht, S., ed. *Massage Manipulation and Traction.* New Haven, CT: Elizabeth Licht Pub., 1960.

3. Mennell, J. B. *Manual Therapy.* Springfield, IL: Charles C. Thomas, 1951.

Stretch to ease muscle strain

By ED BURKE

At one time or another, every cyclist experiences muscle soreness that can be attributed to such things as starting a weight training program, a sudden increase in mileage, an increase in gears and effort, or a change in position on the bike. The pain usually sets in between eight and 24 hours after exercise and is normally gone in a few days.

The commonly held theory attributes the specific soreness to tissue damage, such as microscopic tearing of muscle or connective tissue. This hypothesis was developed by Hough in 1902, but was neither proven by him nor by anyone since then.

Some authorities attribute muscle soreness to incomplete removal of muscle metabolites. Either the production is so great or blood flow is so reduced (or a combination of both) that there is an accumulation of substances that are toxic to the muscles and nerve endings. Such excessive fluid accumulation might account for a swelling of the muscle, making nerve endings more sensitive. This form of muscle stiffness is the type which usually occurs during a long road or stage race. As a result the muscle becomes swollen, shorter and thicker. Light exercise or massage can help reduce this soreness.

Recent work by De Vries has led to the "muscle spasm theory" of delayed localized soreness. The sequence of events may go as follows: 1. the cyclist works out hard; 2. there is a temporary lack of blood flow to the muscle; 3. this ischemia causes pain in nerve endings,

probably activated by the release of a "P substance" across the muscle membrane into the tissue fluid; 4. the pain initiates a reflex toxic muscle contraction (spasm); 5. the spasm prolongs ischemia and the circle is complete.

Much of De Vries' research leads to the use of static stretching to reduce soreness. Electromyographic equipment (which records electrical activity of the muscle) showed less activity in muscles after the use of static stretching. Symptomatic relief seems to parallel lower electromyographic values.

What does De Vries' research mean to cyclists? By following a sound program of warm-up, cool-down and stretching, riders may have a certain degree of control over muscle soreness.

Warming Up

Warming up is associated with increasing muscle temperature, activating energy sources in the muscle, activating hormonal resources, alerting the nervous system, and increasing your body's core temperature. Although very little research has been done on the effect of warm-up and muscle soreness, most people advocate it as a protective measure. Such events as the kilometer and sprint need a better warm-up than those that emphasize endurance. If an active warm-up is impossible, passive warm-up such as massage may be useful.

To train properly and avoid undue soreness, a cyclist must stress his body to the correct degree and then allow it to recover. A progressive program calls for the continual adjustment of the distance and intensity of workouts. When a cyclist is in top shape, adding something new such as weight work, hard intervals, or a change of position on the bike should be done gradually.

Treating Soreness

Muscle soreness can be lessened using one or more of the following treatments.

—Massage. Manipulating the sore muscles after training can help reduce tissue swelling and increase blood flow to remove metabolites.

—Heat. Applying dry or moist heat to the muscles will, like massage, increase blood flow.

—Static stretching. A static exercise program stretches the muscle to its greatest possible length. Stretch the muscle group to the point where you begin to feel the pull, then go a little further and hold the position for about 30 seconds. Avoid sudden or violent stretching (ballistic) which creates a reflex action in the muscle causing it to contract. Static stretching is safer than the ballistic method because it doesn't impose sudden stress upon the tissues involved.

Stretching before and after every ride is most beneficial. If this is impossible, a regular stretching routine should be done daily. A good time to do the exercises is while watching television.

Yoga exercises include many excellent stretching positions. Yoga's exploration of the inner structure of the body and mind may help you discover certain areas of weakness and soreness.

A 15-20 minute stretching routine, as described in the drawings, includes a good assortment of exercises which can help you prevent or control muscle soreness and injury. But remember that any severe muscular pain that lasts for days should receive the attention of your physician.

References

1. Anderson, Bob. *Stretching.* Fullerton, CA: 1975.

2. Anderson, Bob. "The perfect pre-run stretching routine," *Runner's World,* (May 1978).

3. De Vries, H. A. *Physiology of Exercise for Physical Education and Athletics.* Dubuque, IA: William C. Brown Co., 1974.

4. Hough, J. "Ergographic studies in muscular soreness," *Amer. J. Phys.,* No. 7 (1902), p. 76.

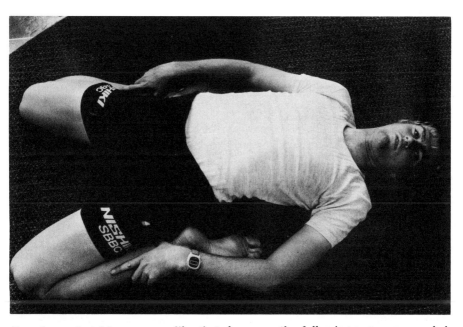

By using a stretching program like that shown on the following pages you can help control muscle soreness and tightness.

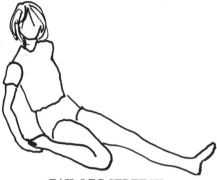

TAIL LEG STRETCH
Sit up with one leg bent directly behind you. Slowly lean back to stretch front of thigh. Hold for 30 seconds, repeat twice for each leg. Excellent stretch for quadriceps.

"V" SIT
Sit with both legs straight and head in line with spine. Bend over straight from hips as far as possible, grabbing legs, ankles or toes. Repeat twice for 30 seconds. Works on hamstrings, lower legs, and lower back.

"J" STRETCH
Lying on your back, lift feet and roll hips over head. Keep legs straight and lower until feet touch floor. (If this is too difficult, then bend knees down to head.) Hold for 30 seconds, relax, and repeat three times. Works on lower back, buttocks, and back of legs.

GASTROCNEMIUS STRETCH
Place rear foot 3-4 feet from wall, keep upper body straight, slowly move hip forward until you feel stretch in straight leg. 30 seconds each leg. Stretches back of leg.

TOE POINTER
Sit on feet, toes and ankles stretched backward. Do not allow toes to angle in and heels to go out. Hold for 30 seconds to one minute. For tightness in front of feet, ankles, knees, and thighs.

LOWER BACK AND BUTTOCKS
Lie on your back, pull one leg toward chest keeping back and head on floor. Hold for 30 seconds and repeat twice with each leg. Stretches buttocks, lower back, and back of thighs.

"L" STRETCH
Lie on floor with buttocks against wall and feet up. Hold from one to five minutes. Increases circulation.

TRUNK TWISTER
With right leg straight, place left foot flat at outside of right knee, reach over outside of left leg, turn head to look over left shoulder. Turn upper body, but not hips. Hold 30 seconds and repeat twice on each side. Stretches back and hip muscles.

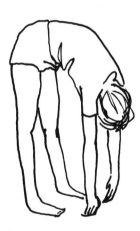

STANDING PASSIVE HANG
From standing position bend over and let body and arms hang, as in touching your toes. Hold for 10-30 seconds, while body settles. Repeat twice. Stretches lower back and hamstrings.

GROIN STRETCH
Lie on your back, bend knees, put soles of feet together, relax, for 30 seconds. Good for lower back and groin muscles.

Drawings by
Jane Swanson

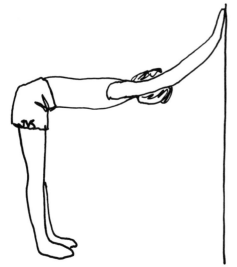

SHOULDERS AND UPPER BACK

With hands on wall at shoulder height, walk backward 3-4 feet keeping feet about one foot apart. Straighten arms, bring spine toward floor and lift buttocks. Hold for 30 seconds or longer. Excellent for upper back and shoulders.

YOGA

Sitting with knees bent and soles of feet together, draw the heels as close to the body as possible, push knees to floor, hold 10 seconds, relax. Repeat 10 times or perform for two minutes at your own pace. Stretches groin and inner thigh muscles.

If you need help, go to an athlete doctor

By ED BURKE

If home remedies can't cope with your injury, you should seek medical help. But where can you go to find the best treatment for an injury resulting from cycling?

There are good reasons why you should seek out a physician who is familiar with sports medicine and the treatment of sports injuries. You may not find one knowledgeable about cycling, but a sports physician understands the physical, psychological and emotional differences between athletes and sedentary individuals.

Many physicians are not familiar with the laboratory test results that an athlete in training will produce. For example, a trained cyclist's blood test may show red cell values which are low for an average individual. Anemia may be the diagnosis. It is now known, however, that athletes actually have an *increased* blood volume from training; the cyclist may even have a higher number of red blood cells than a sedentary individual. But the increased blood volume lowered the concentration of cells, making the rider appear somewhat anemic.

Many physicians are not aware that injuries to athletes such as cyclists often require non-standard treatments. Furthermore, some treatments that produce good results with non-athletes may have an adverse effect on cyclists. The use of cortisone to help ease tendon inflammation is common. But cortisone reduces the blood supply to the tendons, and if an athlete were to work the muscle tendon maximally there is a greater possibility of tearing it.

I recommend that you search for a physician who is also an athlete. He or she may have had problems similar to yours. Call the local high school or college trainer and ask for names of physicians experienced in treating athletic injuries. There is also the possibility of the trainer offering to help you. Contact the nearest medical school; it will have contacts with physicians who work with athletes.

If all else fails, call the local chapter of the American Medical Association for information. If the local chapter is not listed, contact the main office at 535 N. Dearborn St., Chicago, IL 60610.

If your injury involves bone or muscle, contact a sports orthopedist. To find those closest to you contact the American Orthopaedic Society of Sports Medicine, 430 N. Michigan Ave., Chicago, IL 60611.

Chronic problems associated with the legs and feet should be examined by a sports podiatrist. If you cannot find one, contact the sources of information listed above. Ask for those who are members of the American Academy of Podiatric Sports Medicine.

Though the number of doctors and related personnel in sports medicine is small, the specialty is growing and the future looks very bright for the athlete. I also see benefits for the physicians who work with athletes. A better knowledge of rehabilitative principles and methods will help doctors return any patient to health more quickly, and close contacts with school-age athletes will keep them "in tune" with the younger generation.

If a physician is interested in working with cycling, a local coach or club will likely greet the idea with enthusiasm. Any medical person can gain important experience this way. Much information about treatment of sports injuries is becoming available in seminars across the country and in books and magazines (e.g. *The Physician and Sports Medicine*).

If a physician is thinking of getting involved in sports medicine for the financial rewards he can forget it. Office and emergency visits are covered by health insurance, but travel, advice about health care, extra time spent with local athletes, and other time-consuming items are not. Sports medicine means being involved, having interest, and giving time and effort. The specialty is open to those aggressive enough to undertake its challenge.

Questions

Questions cyclists ask most

By ED BURKE

During the last two years, I have had the opportunity to conduct many USCF clinics around the country. Below are many of the questions asked numerous times by cyclists. You may also have some of these questions. I hope the answers will add some insight to your problems and help your riding.

Q. Why do some athletes who use carbohydrate loading sometimes gain weight and experience muscle stiffness?

A. While carbohydrate loading is an excellent way to increase the body's stores of energy fuel, water is also accumulated. With each gram of glycogen, an average of three grams of water is stored. This extra water storage in the muscles tends to give you a sense of heaviness or stiffness.

During carbohydrate loading the athlete tends to cut back in training while continuing to eat at a normal pace. Consequently, weight is gained. However, in endurance exercise, the benefits of extra energy from glycogen stores offset the extra weight. In hot weather the extra water may also compensate for water loss from sweating.

Q. What effect does vitamin B-15 have on performance?

A. B-15 is a water soluble nutrient which is not recognized in the United States as a vitamin. It can be purchased in many health food stores in the form of calcium- or sodium-pangamic acid.

Good natural sources are brewers yeast, whole brown rice, whole grains, and sesame seeds.

Pangamic acid has received much attention due to the claim that it aids in the uptake of oxygen by the cells and that it can stimulate glucose oxidation. While many tests have been conducted with B-15 in the USSR on patients with cancer, asthma and heart disease, very little research has been conducted in the U.S. If you are eating a diet poor in B-vitamins and grains, maybe supplementation with B-15 will be of benefit. But if this is the case then you should also take a full B-complex supplement.

Q. When I have minor abrasions and lacerations should I allow a scab to form?

A. A scab is nature's way of providing protection from infection. However, nature was around before cycling was invented. In cycling, a scab can reopen before healing is complete. And if the scab is on a joint, range of motion may be impeded.

After the wound has been thoroughly cleaned, a petroleum-base medicated ointment should be applied and covered with a nonadhering sterile pad. Ideally, wounds should then heal from the inside out. By changing the dressing daily, new tissue has a chance to form. Studies have shown that wounds heal quicker when they are covered with a dressing than when a scab is allowed to form.

Q. During the race what can be done to relieve muscle cramping?

A. Muscle cramping can be the result of one or more causes: lack of fluids, insufficient electrolyte (mineral) balance, cold weather, poor circulation, muscle and nerve fatigue. Immediately you should try to stretch the muscle. For example, if the spasm is located in the right calf, stand on the pedals and lower the right heel. Next, massage the calf with one hand and drink some fluids.

That evening, replace your lost fluids with an electrolyte drink and add some extra salt to your food. Muscle cramping may also be a sign that more conditioning is needed.

Q. After an accident, how long should cold be administered to a muscle contusion?

A. Immediate application of cold packs or ice with slight pressure from an elastic wrap will help control internal bleeding and pain. Swelling will also stay down, and chances are good that you will be able to return to training and racing sooner. Cold acts to constrict blood vessels and to numb sensory nerve endings. But extreme cold must be avoided so that tissue damage does not result.

You will see the immediate benefits of cold in reduced swelling. Swelling may subside in 24 hours for some injuries; others may take over 72 hours. There is no rule on when to discontinue cold in favor of heat. It will depend on your preferences and nature of injury. When you choose to use heat, make sure not to overheat the skin. Never begin heat treatment until hemorrhaging has stopped.

Q. What can be done to prevent Montezuma's Revenge while racing in a foreign country?

A. The cause of diarrhea is often difficult to establish. It is conceivable that any irritant may cause a loose stool. This can include either an infestation of parasitic organisms or an emotional upset. In a foreign land where the water may be contaminated or food slightly spoiled it is easy to encounter such problems.

Many over-the-counter preparations can be bought such as Kaopectate and Pepto-Bismol. Prescription drugs such as Lomotil will also stop bowel movements. Doctors lately have reported in the *New England Journal of Medicine* that this is highly effective in easing the symptoms of diarrhea. But it advises against using the drug for longer than three weeks until more tests are done. The drug may also have an adverse effect on athletic performance.

Q. Would I increase the amount of protein in my diet during hard training?

A. While muscle is composed of protein, it does not break down to provide energy for pedaling a bicycle. Hard exercise depletes the muscle of its stores of carbohydrate (glycogen) and fat, not protein. An athlete in hard training needs to consume only about 2-2.5 grams of protein per kilogram (2.2 pounds) of body weight. For example, a 70 kilogram athlete needs to consume 160 to 175 grams (5-7 ounces) of quality protein per day to maintain protein balance.

You should eat a balanced protein diet of meat, fish, grains and dairy products to ensure receiving all the essential amino acids. A general rule of thumb to follow in diet planning is to consume your daily calories in the following proportions: 60% carbohydrates, 25% fat, 15% protein.

Q. A coach once said that a cyclist has different muscles than other athletes and there's no need to do stretching exercises if you are fit. Is this true?

A. It has been shown that hard exercise shortens muscles and makes them more prone to injury from pulls or strains. Many athletes today use static stretching and yoga exercises as an integral part of their training program. It is also advisable in the middle of a long stage race to lower your seat 2-3mm to compensate for this problem.

As for cyclists having different muscles than other athletes, nothing could be further from the truth. A cyclist's muscles become tired and tense like those of any other athlete, and stretching along with massage will help speed recovery. Remember, a tight muscle is more susceptible to injury.

Q. Many people still advocate that a cyclist should only drink one bottle of water or less in a 100 kilometer race, even when the temperature is over 100F degrees. Is this good thinking?

A. While most well-trained cyclists could probably do well in a 100 kilometer race on one bottle, I believe that most of the time they will do worse than their potential. From research we know that the heart must work harder when a state of dehydration is near, and your internal temperature will be higher. Just think what effect this will have on performance. Heart rate alone is about 10 beats a minute higher in the dehydrated state.

Drinking fluids will minimize the degree of dehydration which results from racing, thereby reducing the heart rate and internal temperature. Studies have shown that with steady fluid replacement more blood is available for the transport of oxygen and food to the muscles, as well as for carrying away heat. Based on these simple facts I think it is very wise to drink a little fluid every few minutes during the race.

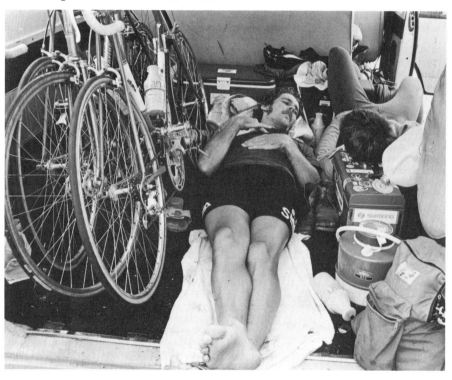

Ask Ed Burke

EDITOR'S NOTE: Physiologist Ed Burke has a column in Velo-news *in which he responds to questions sent in by readers. Though the questions come from individuals, the replies often contain information which may be of interest to other cyclists. The following is a selection from that column, "Ask Ed Burke."*

Can a racing cyclist donate a pint of blood, drink plenty of fluids, and then resume training two or three days later and still have the same ability to transport oxygen via the blood as he had before giving blood (and after the blood is replaced by the body)? If not, how long is it until you get back to where you were?

In a study conducted by Ekblom (Jour. Appl. Physio., 1972, 175-180) 800ml of blood was drawn from athletes to observe its effects on certain physiological variables. The results showed that heart rate was elevated at submaximal workloads, and that total work capacity was decreased by 30 percent the next day. It took an average of 14 days for the subject to reach pre-experiment values.

Blood plasma (mostly water) will come back to normal in a few days, but red cell formation will take longer. Training may be continued during this time, but maximal performance will be reduced. Training will also stimulate erthropoiesis, or red blood cell formation.

To my knowledge the blood type has no effect on the oxygen carrying capacity of the blood. Abnormal hemoglobin may cause anemia such as sickle cell anemia. Sickle cell anemia has a severe effect on the transport of red blood cells in the small blood vessels.

Much has already been written about the general benefits of moderate wine consumption among all adults. My question: Does wine have any specific value to the serious cyclist, such as replacement of compounds lost in sweating or respiration? I'm referring here to consumption after racing or training.

Wine and other alcoholic beverages, when taken in moderation, should have no detrimental effect on an athlete. Results of contemporary research indicate that an acute ingestion (one or two glasses a day) has little or no effect upon general or cardiovascular endurance.

In fact, I have known some marathon runners who drink 6 to 10 beers a day with no adverse effects. Wine and beer are served during the main meal at most major races in Europe.

Wine is an excellent source of calories. One gram yields seven calories and may help replace some of the minerals lost during hard training and racing.

Sometimes after a hard jam or while climbing a steep hill, I receive a sharp pain in my side just below the ribs. Is there any way to prevent this "stitch," and what can be done during the race to relieve the agony?

"Stitch" is a term used to describe a number of internal pains that occur near the bottom of the rib cage. This stabbing pain is still something of a mystery to physiologists and doctors, who have come up with several theories as to its causes.

Because it usually occurs during an increase in metabolic demands, it may be caused by lack of oxygen to the muscles used in heavy breathing (diaphragm and intercostal muscles). Lack of oxygen to any working muscle causes pain and discomfort.

Inherent weakness of the diaphragm or unaccustomed stretching of muscles between the ribs caused by heavy breathing may be the problem in some unconditioned cyclists. As with any muscles that are inadequately trained, these can become badly fatigued during heavy breathing, leading to impaired respiratory performance and cramping.

Performing deep breathing exercises may build up the strength of these muscles. Training under the same breathing conditions as in a race may at least develop a tolerance to the pain. A conditioning program which includes stretching exercises aimed at breathing muscles may be excellent preventative medicine.

I have heard a report that some physiologists and distance runners look down on bicycle racing as a means for attaining fitness. If one runs at a pace to keep his/her pulse at a certain level is that more beneficial than cycling with a similar pulse?

Cycling is a poor means of obtaining fitness unless you know how to train properly. Too many tend to quit and coast when they feel fatigue. As a consequence their heart rates do not rise high enough for physical benefit.

Remember also that you must work harder on the bike to obtain the same heart rate as in running, because of the smaller muscle mass used in cycling.

If you run or cycle at identical heart rates, then you are stressing the cardiovascular system to the same degree. This is true because of a direct relationship between heart rate and oxygen consumption: as heart rate increases, oxygen consumption increases.

When you can ride a good pace long enough to stress the heart continuously, then cycling is an excellent form of exercise. One advantage riding has over distance running is less stress on the knee, ankle and foot joints.

Is there any value to eating quick energy food before a race? For example, I've seen some riders eating large amounts of honey or candy bars approximately 30 minutes before the race.

Several studies have shown that a sugar feeding 30-40 minutes before competition tends to drive the blood sugar levels very high, causing a hypoglycemic response (low blood sugar) that can be devastating to a cyclist's performance.

There is a large increase of sugar in the blood after ingestion, but this is accompanied by an increase in plasma insulin levels above levels of normal exercising. Insulin, a hormone released by the pancreas in response to high blood glucose levels, helps transport sugars out of the blood. Consequently, the cyclist will most likely have lower blood glucose levels than if he had not ingested sugar.

The brain and central nervous system function primarily on blood glucose and these organs may not perform at maximum because of lower fuel stores. These physiological responses may last 30-60 minutes into the race and lead up to the "bonk" later on.

Quick energy foods are another one of those myths that cyclists should investigate before believing.

I've been racing in this country for almost five years, and several years in another country. One of my biggest problems is my breathing. At the first races of the year it's very difficult to sustain my breathing, up to the point that I have to stop racing in order to breathe normally. If by any chance I finish with the group, I won't be able to sprint because I am so suffocated that I have to finish very slow. Regardless of my preparation, nothing works for me; I still have the same problem. I've been to doctors but they don't find anything wrong with me. Do you think I don't have enough oxygen in my blood, or do you think I don't have enough stamina?

The medical community would describe your difficult, labored and uncomfortable breathing as dyspnea. This results in an excess buildup of carbon dioxide in the blood and a reduction of oxygen content. At least three factors can cause this problem:

1. Lack of oxygen in the blood. This can result from anemia or by hypoventilation due to airway passage blockage, as seen in individuals with asthma.

2. Increased discharge of impulses from the respiratory control center in the brain which inhibit the respiratory muscles. This has been referred to as the Hering Breuer Reflex.

3. Dyspnea may be experienced because of an abnormal state of mind (emotional dyspnea).

If consultation with your doctor and a specialist in respiratory diseases does not produce any results, I suggest you take a hard look at your cycling program. You should incorporate intervals into your training to develop your tolerance to lactic acid and oxygen debt. Concentrate on the rate and depth of your breathing, which should be deep enough to insure adequate turnover of air in the lungs.

Recent research conducted with athletes exercising at near-maximal levels showed that a rate of 30 to 35 breaths per minute is more efficient than faster or slower rates. This optimal rate seems to be most effective in gas exchange between lungs and blood.

Are there any colleges currently teaching exercise physiology, sports medicine, or sports training in reference to cycling that offer M.S./Ph.D. programs?

The study of exercise and sports physiology is concerned with individuals under stress of muscular activity. This stress can range from manual labor performed under adverse environmental conditions to riding a 100 mile road race. Today more than ever before it is necessary for the athlete and coach to utilize the vital role science can play in the successful development of training programs.

Before entering a Masters or Ph.D. program in exercise physiology a student should have a good science background as an undergraduate. A typical curriculum combination might be a major in biology or chemistry with a physical education minor. As more and more research is conducted at the cellular level the importance of a good science background increases. An interested student who lacks study in organic chemistry or biochemistry can usually take these courses while working on a Masters.

Listed below are several universities which offer a Masters degree or a Ph.D. in exercise physiology. For further information contact the department chairman.

-University of Arizona, Dept. of Physical Education, Tucson, AZ 85721.

-University of Iowa, Physical Education Dept., Iowa City, IA 52240.

-University of California, Dept. of Kinesiology, Los Angeles, CA 90024.

-University of Massachusetts, Dept. of Sports Science, Amherst, MA 01002.

-Ball State University, Human Performance Laboratory, Muncie, IN 47306.

-Ohio State University, Dept. of Health & Physical Education, Work Physiology Lab, 337 West 17th St., Columbus, OH 43210.

-Florida State University, Dept. of Physical Education, Montgomery Gym, Tallahassee, FL 32306.

-University of Michigan, Physical Education Dept., Ann Arbor, MI 48109.

I am inquiring about back pains which my son developed while competing in cyclocross. He was checked by a doctor, x-rays were taken, and it was concluded that the problem was stretched tendons in the lower back. The pain became so severe that he was forced to take a two-month layoff. I would appreciate some information on "preventive maintenance" that can stop back problems from happening in the future.

More than half the people of the United States will suffer from some form of back pain in their lifetime. The back, and particularly the spine, is such a complex area (over 100 muscles involved) that many physicians have a hard time diagnosing the source of the pain.

Back problems may be hereditary, such as sway back or scoliosis, or they can be the result of a fall from the bike. Sometimes pain may subside in a few days only to reappear later. More often than not, most back problems are the result of poor posture,

lack of stretching or flexibility, and lack of muscular strength of the stomach and back.

Exercises which can help strengthen the abdominal and gluteal muscles and improve flexibility of the hip are pictured. Perform the exercises for at least three periods of 30 seconds each, with rest between stretches. Stretch to a point where you are feeling an easy pull and try to stay relaxed. These are not cure-alls for every low back pain, but they should help many people.

Use both hands to gently pull leg toward chest (alternate legs).

Squat and bend forward, dropping head and arms between knees.

Support lower back with hands.

Bent knee sit-ups with feet free, which isolates stomach muscles.

Reach forward and hold onto legs.

Alternately bring opposite knee and elbow together.

On rides over 20 miles I have a problem with numbness in my left foot. It starts in the area of the small toe and gradually works in to the area from the ball of the foot forward. At first I thought it was due to a tight shoe, but a switch to a wide shoe did nothing to relieve the symptom.

There is also a problem with my right foot. After long rides involving hills I have pain and swelling on the ball of the foot behind the large toe and in the joint of the large toe. When riding, I can feel what seems to be a bunching of the flesh on the bottom of the foot in the joint area of the large toe.

The constant pressure on the balls of the feet from pedaling can cause a weak or fallen anterior metatarsal arch. This arch lies under the ball of the foot, behind the second and third toes.

When supporting tissues, ligaments and muscles lose their ability to support the long bones of the foot (metatarsal heads) in a dome-like shape, a falling of the arch occurs. This places pressure on the nerve and blood vessels in the area. You would first notice an irritation and redness on the ball of the foot. As the condition progresses there is an increase in pain, toe cramping, and often a burning sensation develops.

Care of the fallen anterior metatarsal arch requires light massage and metatarsal pads (quarter-inch felt cut to two-inch circumference).

Place a pad under the rear part of the ball of the foot and fix it in place with 2-3 strips of tape. If the problem continues, consult a sports podiatrist.

It has been my understanding that drinking cold fluids is not good for the body, especially during strenuous activity. Is there any truth or logic to this?

The comments you've heard are primarily myth and maybe just a little fact. In general, there is no particular harm caused to the stomach from drinking cold water. As a matter of fact, on very hot days when you are overheating and need water replacement, cold fluids (45-55F degrees) are helpful since they also help cool the body.

Fluids must pass from the stomach into the intestine before entering the blood. Studies conducted by Costill and Saltin (*Journal of Applied Physiology* 37(5):679-683) found that cold drinks empty more rapidly than warm fluids. Lower temperature increases the activity of the stomach wall, causing a more rapid flow into the intestine.

None of the studies reported cases of stomach cramps. Gastric distress is probably more related to the volume consumed than its temperature. During competition you should drink 4-5 ounces of the cold fluid every 10-15 minutes.

While it is possible to increase your aerobic potential, is there any evidence that training will increase short-term energy supplies?

Training can increase the maximal amount of energy supplied by the aerobic system (oxygen consumption) by approximately 20-25 percent. The degree of improvement is more limited for anaerobic sources (ATP-CP and lactic acid systems) responsible for high intensity efforts.

Because of this, champion athletes are born, not made. Per-Olaf Astrand, a famous Swedish exercise physiologist, once stated, "If you want to be a champion athlete, pick your parents carefully."

However, while improvements are limited, long-term training will improve any athlete. You will be able to better utilize any energy sources and work closer to your maximal level without being fatigued. With training, the non-fatigue level may increase from 60 to 90 percent of maximum, even if the important factor in energy expenditure is mainly genetic.

I'm 33 years old, 6-foot-1 and weigh 190lbs. In 1972 I started riding to lose weight and to acquire some fitness. I weighed 240lbs then and had competed in high school and college as a running back, wrestler and on the track. In 1976 I decided to become competitive on a bicycle and my O_2 level at that time tested at 55.7ml/min. I progressed to become a Senior I by July of '77 and have averaged about 9,000 miles of training and racing for the last three years. Last September I was again tested on the ergometer and my O_2 level was 67ml/min.

My questions: 1. Without the facility to be tested as to muscle fiber, what type of event should I be racing? (My personal bests are a 1:18 kilo, a 5:40 pursuit, a 12.6 200m, a 1:03 25-mile time trial.) 2. If you suggest track and criterium, what can I do to improve my speed? 3. Should I specialize at this time? So far I've just ridden to compete.

None of my accomplishments in cycling are exceptional, but I think I have the determination, desire and drive to do very well at the district and possibly national level. Any information and suggestions for me will be greatly appreciated.

For someone who is training 9,000 miles a year, is 33 years old and has a maximal oxygen consumption of 67ml, I would say you have trained to your physiological maximum. Looking at your times for the track events, I don't believe you can lower your kilometer time by 10 seconds or your pursuit time by one minute. This is what it would take to become a national-class cyclist in these events.

While I would not discourage you from competing on the track, I would say your chances of finding success would be in road races and criteriums. Since you have an above-average maximal oxygen consumption level and this type of racing is mostly aerobic, your strength probably lies here.

You don't seem to have problems finding time to train nor do you lack determination. By setting some realistic goals for yourself and by directing your training toward those goals, success will come. Who knows—I may even see you at this year's national road race!

I work out three times weekly using the Nautilus program. My strength increase and weight decrease (2,500 calories daily) was dramatic until I reached 200 lbs. Now, due to a low energy level because of the dieting, I am progressing very slowly on strength increase. My questions: Should I continue to work on my upper body and therefore build muscle and more weight? Can I build enough strength to be competitive against my fellow Veterans, seeing as how I seem to have to carry 200 lbs. on my 6-foot-1 frame? When should upper body strength be a consideration in cycling?

From your description of how you feel at your present weight it may be wise for you to maintain your present caloric intake. Increasing your energy output with riding will probably continue to burn up those excess pounds of fat.

Any form of weight training should be used as a supplement to your on-the-bike training. You want to be able to develop enough upper body strength to climb more efficiently, and to stabilize your body when sprinting.

With a proper program you will be able to develop strength and endurance with-out putting on the bulk of a weight lifter. Three sets of six-to-eight repetitions with a weight you can handle tends to develop both strength and endurance. Too much weight lifting may tend to put on pounds of muscle which may be detrimental to your performance in certain events.

Once you have reached a desired level of strength, a maintenance program should be used throughout the season. Exercising with weights once or twice a week at near maximal contractions will maintain strength and endurance.

What are the latest findings on pre-competition meals for road racing?

There are several types of pre-competition meals being used in athletics these days. The best diet provides modest amounts of carbohydrate foods, taken in at least two hours before the event. If instead a high protein/fat meal is eaten, it will take about 5-10% more oxygen to metabolize and will be slow in emptying from the stomach. In addition, a low carbohydrate meal will fail to supplement the glucose necessary for immediate energy. A pre-race meal including items like juice, pancakes, rice, toast, honey, fruit and tea would fulfill necessary requirements.

The use of liquid meals is becoming more popular with athletes. Such products as Ensure (Ross Laboratories) can satisfy the pre-race needs of cyclists. They are high in carbohydrates, come in several flavors, aid in hydration, and empty from the stomach quickly. Many athletes who have a hard time digesting a solid meal due to a nervous stomach, will experience no nausea, vomiting, or stomach cramps from these products.

A proper pre-event meal should provide enough energy to minimize hunger and fatigue, and above all, it should be something you like to eat.

Looking at pictures of the East German track riders, I notice that they are very muscular. Is there a relationship between muscular size and strength? Will a cyclist with big muscles lose the ability to spin?

Physiologists see a definite relationship between the size of a muscle and its strength. The larger the cross area of a muscle the greater force it can produce — increase one factor and the other also increases.

Often, however, we see an athlete who has large muscles but cannot produce as much strength as an individual with smaller muscles. Some confusion here can be explained by the fact that muscle strength is also governed by such things as bodily proportions (leverage), neurological efficiency and skill in performing the movement. This is why it is almost impossible to accurately compare the pure muscular strength of two individuals.

The best thing for a cyclist to do is keep accurate performance records over a period of time. Then you will know if you are really becoming stronger, regardless of any changes in muscle size.

The ability of an athlete to do skill tasks is not adversely affected by muscle size, and you will not lose the ability to spin on the bicycle as muscles grow. This is proven by those East Germans you mentioned and by numerous other powerfully built—and fast—riders.

Here's a question I have been trying to find out for two years with different answers from different people only making me more confused. Does Saturday racing have an effect on Sunday's performance?

Saturday racing will have an effect on fuel stores of the muscles. If you were to have a hard race on Saturday the concentration of glycogen (stored glucose) may be drastically reduced in the working musculature. Even if the Saturday evening meal contained roughly 60 percent carbohydrate, the muscle levels would not come back to prerace levels.

Recently a Scandinavian study has shown that following prolonged exhaustive exercise young men require approximately 46 hours to restore muscle glycogen to pre-exercise levels. This was in spite of the fact that the subjects ate a diet containing 90 percent carbohydrates.

This is not to say you should never race two or more days in a row; just think what would happen to the Tour de France if they had a rest day every other day. Trained cyclists have a higher capacity to use fat to produce energy, which is improved by their long distance training. This has a tendency to spare some muscle glycogen.

A cyclist with a very important race would be wise to ride easily for the two days before. This will insure adequate stores of glycogen.

What can you tell me about flat feet and cycling? I have very flexible flat feet which bang all over the place whenever I climb a mountain and stand up. Would you say I have weak ankles? What would be a good exercise to remedy this? What can I do to improve my bicycling performance in regard to my feet and ankles?

Flat feet can be caused by a variety of stresses which weaken the ligaments and muscles which support the long arch of the foot. A cyclist will usually complain of tiredness and tenderness in the arch and heel.

This condition may result from poorly fitting shoes, weakened supportive tissue, overweight, anatomical abnormalities, or overuse which subjects the arch to undue strain.

Care includes the correct size shoes, arch supports, and 2-3 supportive strips of tape directly around the arch. If the problem is more severe, visit a sports podiatrist for advice and look into having orthotics (corrective inserts) made for you.

Exercises which will help strengthen the arches and ankles are: toe raises, walking on the inside and outside of your feet, picking up marbles with your toes, flexion and extension of the foot with added resistance, and massage.

The best long-range treatment for all foot abnormalities, whether anatomical or acquired, appears to be the use of corrective inserts.

Is there any way that a rider can determine his heart rate while he is riding? Taking one's pulse while riding seems difficult. Is there a way that one could monitor heart rate, or possibly determine it in some other way?

You can determine your heart rate while cycling from the carotid artery, a large artery in your neck just under your jaw bone and beside your Adam's apple. You can mount a watch to the handlebars, use one hand to find the artery and then count the beats for 10 seconds. Then multiply the 10-second count by six to determine your heart beats per minute. If you have difficulty counting while pedaling, coast for the 10 seconds.

Those looking for a more sophisticated means of observing heart rate may wish to purchase a pocket size heart rate monitor. With the use of this instrument, you can maintain your heart rate within a preselected range. Two firms which market these instruments are: Respironics Inc., 650 Seco Road, Monroeville, PA 15146; and, Amerec Corp., Fitness Equipment Div., Box 3825, Bellevue, WA 98009.

For example, you may wish to exercise at an intensity which raises the heart rate to a range of 150-160 beats per minute. Once this range is set, the monitor will automatically alarm if your heart rate goes outside boundaries.

I would be very interested in knowing how cycle training affects blood pressure.

Blood pressure is the driving force that moves the blood through your body. The highest pressure is obtained when the heart contracts and is called systolic pressure. The lowest pressure occurs while the heart is filling and is called diastolic pressure.

During cycling, blood pressure increases as a result of the volume of blood being pumped by the heart (cardiac output). This affects systolic pressure more than diastolic pressure. The reason is that there is a decrease in resistance in the blood system because more capillaries open to supply blood to the working muscles. This means that more blood drains from the arteries and into the muscle capillaries, thus minimizing changes in diastolic pressure.

Following training, blood pressure at the same absolute work load is lower than before training. In other words, if you ride at the same speed after a period of training as you did before you began training, your blood pressure for that particular speed would be lower. Also, people with a condition of high blood pressure will show reductions in resting diastolic and systolic blood pressure with training.

In an attempt to increase my overall muscular strength for next year, I started my winter weight training program about four weeks ago (lifting three times per week). Since I've started I've felt weak on the bike and my weekly TT times have gone up. Do you think I should not worry about it and just ride easy when lifting? Should I do workouts on the bike that increase strength and lift only when the weather keeps me off the bike? I'm 21 years old and in my third year of racing; I weigh 163 pounds and stand 6-foot-3. I need more horsepower for the hills!

Cyclists involved in any activity in which they are trying to improve their level of fitness should investigate the concept of quality vs. quantity. It is my contention that most cyclists could decrease their quantity of work considerably and continue to produce the same results. The implication is that many athletes perform too much exercise and don't allow their bodies to fully recover.

The body is only capable of recovering from a certain amount of exercise. Too much expenditure of energy will not allow full recuperation, and if such over-expenditure continues then the cyclist's level of fitness will gradually decrease. If the body is not allowed to complete the rebuilding phase of training due to lack of rest or nutrition, then the destruction will eventually exceed the body's ability to repair itself.

I recommend that you continue the strength training, but re-evaluate your program. Are you expending too much energy in this program, which ultimately will affect your riding? You need to find the right balance between strength training, on the bike training, and *rest*!

After a hard training session, things like light stretching, meditation, sauna, a nap, or massage will aid the regeneration process. Liberal doses of these activities can quicken healing and rebuilding.

I would like to see some information about knee problems often occurring in bicyclists (esp. tendinitis).What are the causes? What are the preventions? What do you do when you get a knee problem and how can you stay in shape with a bad knee? Are people prone to keep getting tendinitis once they have had it? These are just some questions of interest to many cyclists I'm sure.

Most knee problems in cycling are associated with the tendons of the knee joint. A tendon is connective tissue that attaches muscle to bone. A tendon can become inflamed, usually at a point where it attaches to the bone or joint, and we have a condition referred to as tendinitis.

The causes of tendinitis in cycling are often non-specific, but continuous activity of the muscle and tendon is thought to be the problem. Many cyclists complain of tendinitis after too many early-season miles, pushing big gears, or improper position of the shoe cleat.

The first principle of treatment is rest to the injured knee. This will allow any microscopic tears or inflammation to subside. To ensure this rest, some doctors will suggest that the cyclist curtail riding for a while.

Many athletes take aspirin and apply cold packs as anti-inflammatory steps, while some go the more radical approach of cortisone injections. However, there is medical evidence to indicate that while cortisone injections will reduce the pain and inflammation, they may interfere with the normal healing process. Many physicians are divided over the use of cortisone injections at all, while some athletes have received repeated injections without any complications.

After rest has helped inflammation to subside, the cyclist should remember that some atrophy has occurred to the muscles of the leg. Go easy until the muscles have been re-exercised back to normal strength.

I have been a racing cyclist more or less continuously since 1965 with some successes, particularly on the track and in short road races, but on occasion in events as long as 100 miles. I am also a diabetic, a condition I presently control solely by dietary means. Generally, I am unable to predict my performance at distances over 40 miles, regardless of preparation on the bike. Physicians I have questioned are unable to offer any encouragement. I have heard of a Dutch professional rider who was successful despite being a diabetic during his career. This would indicate there exist means to diminish the handicap, possibly by a unified program of diet and training. Can you shed any light on this?

There are two kinds of diabetes. One has its onset in childhood and is termed juvenile diabetes. It is often severe and complicated. Diabetes that develops late in life (maturity onset diabetes) is mild and usually occurs in obese people.

The cause of diabetes can be lack of insulin production or the blockage of glucose (fuel to the muscles) from entering the cell. Insulin is a hormone produced in the pancreas and its single basic effect is to increase the rate of glucose transport through membranes of cells. Without glucose the energy production of the cell is altered for the worse. Diabetics control their condition by insulin injections or by adjusting their diets. In most cases of adult onset diabetes the condition can be controlled by diet.

Exercise can also be used in the control of diabetes, although it frequently has the opposite effect on insulin required by the diabetic, reducing it considerably below what is needed. But increased muscular activity increases the transport of glucose into the muscle cells even in the absence of insulin. Thus, exercise actually has an insulin-like effect. Often the person with severe diabetes requires less insulin to control the condition if he or she is living an active life.

So, the diabetic cyclist functions while exercising more like an athlete with a healthy pancreas. There should either be a reduction of supplementary insulin or an increase in the intake of carbohydrates during riding.

I was diagnosed by my orthopedic doctor as having mild chondromalacia. I developed the problem one week after finishing fourth in a 125-mile race in June and was unable to ride for the rest of the season. My orthopedic doctor said that there were no exercises possible when I asked him what I could do for the knee, so you've really given me new life when you said such a condition can be improved by strengthening the quadriceps (*Velo-news*, Dec. 8, 1978). Could you please outline a quadricep program that can help me ride again?

Some cyclists have excessive pronation of the foot, which may cause knee pain. This excessive pronation exaggerates the normal twisting inward of the lower leg when force is applied to the pedals. This causes the kneecap to rub painfully against the long bone of the thigh. Foot pads or orthotics may prevent the excessive pronation and let you pedal without pain.

Weakness in the ligaments and tendons which surround the knee can also cause excessive movement of the knee joint. Strength training exercises for the quadriceps, hamstrings and calf muscles will help make the knee more

stable. Knee extension and flexion exercises, leg presses and calf raises with weights should be worked into your program.

It might be wise to have a qualified coach examine your position on the bike. If your seat is too low it will cause stress on the kneecap. Also, the position of your foot on the pedal may be creating torsion on your lower leg, causing the kneecap to rub.

Several years back, Dave Boll had problems with his knees which orthopedic doctors could not seem to cure. A simple adjustment to his shoe cleats was all that was needed.

Recently, on the advice of a friend, I have begun to supplement my diet with B vitamins in the hope for improved performance and recovery. Does an extremely high B vitamin diet have a beneficial or damaging effect on athletes?

In general each of the B vitamins is essential for the metabolism of carbohydrates and fats. Contrary to what many people think, vitamins are not a food source for energy — they promote reactions concerned with the breakdown of food into useful energy (ATP). The B vitamins need the basic food groups to act upon; otherwise they are useless.

It has been suggested that daily requirements for B vitamins increase with the energy output of the cyclist. But since the caloric intake of the rider should also be increasing, it is likely that greater amounts of foods rich in B vitamins will be consumed, making additional supplements unnecessary.

However, an inexpensive B-complex supplement may be taken as a safeguard. At the present time, it appears that even massive doses of B vitamins have no significant toxic effect — they are water soluble and are not stored in the body.

Natural sources of B vitamins include brewers yeast, wheat germ, most wholegrain cereals such as wheat, rice and oats, seeds and nuts, soybeans, milk products, vegetables such as beets, potatoes and leafy greens.

I suffer from a chronic pain, tenderness and a catching or clicking sensation in my knee. Some people have suggested I have chondromalacia. What is this injury and what may I do to cure the problem?

Chondromalacia is a degenerative process that results in a softening of the under surface of the knee cap. It is usually caused by a minor or severe injury to the knee, or by some inherent softening of the knee cap without any known reason.

Protection must be given in the form of shock absorbing pads and an extensive quadriceps conditioning program. A cortisone injection may be administered to reduce the pain and inflammation, but this may interfere with the normal healing process. You may also wish to increase your intake of calcium and phosphorus to help in the process of bone formation.

Weight training and isometric exercises which concentrate on the quadriceps muscles will do wonders in reconditioning the knee cap and supporting structure.

If the problem continues, see a good orthopedic surgeon. Neglect will cause destruction of the bone and cartilage and result in an arthritic condition.

The day after last year's national time trial the muscles in my thighs were tight and sore. Several cyclists suggested this was lactic acid. If this was the problem what could I have done to relieve it?

The pain felt in muscles the day after an event is not from lactic acid stores, but rather from swelling in overstressed muscle cells and microscopic muscle tearing.

Within an hour after a hard ride (which will most likely produce large amounts of lactic acid) 99% of the lactate has been removed from the working muscles and converted into other products. Ten percent of the lactic acid removed during the immediate recovery period is converted to blood glucose and 75% is used by your aerobic system as a fuel. The remaining 15% probably goes to the liver and is converted into liver glycogen (stored glucose).

The latent soreness was most likely caused by microscopic tears to new muscle cells that were used for the first time to push the big gear. Fluid had moved into the muscle fibers causing a swelling which you sensed as soreness, tenderness and pain. Rest and easy pedaling will help mend the injured cells, while massage will remove the fluids from the swollen muscle fibers and stimulate the lymphatic system to remove metabolic waste products.

What type and color of clothing should a cyclist wear in hot, sunny weather?

I have wondered for a long time why cyclists wear dark colored clothing in hot, sunny weather. Dark colors absorb the sun's rays and can elevate the body's temperature. This problem is most evident in such races as the Red Zinger, where the race is conducted between 5,000 and 11,000 feet above sea level and solar radiation is increased.

I have suggested for several years that the U.S. national team jersey be changed to white with red and blue horizontal stripes.

Along with light color, the jersey should be made of breathable fabric, such as wool, which can wick moisture away from the skin. This will aid in the dissipation of heat from the body while exercising. Wearing a white hat may also be of some benefit.

What precautions can be taken by athletes to keep jet lag to a minimum when traveling cross-country or overseas to race?

For many athletes such travel induces physiological stress which results in a syndrome identified as "circadian dysrhythmia." This reflects a desynchronization of your biological time clock. Body mechanisms such as temperature, metabolism, sleep, and hormone production adapt at varying rates to time changes.

Symptoms may include one or more of the following: insomnia, headache, dizziness, and extreme fatigue. One or more days of easy activity may be needed to aid recovery. Catlett (*Modern Medicine*, 36:1970) suggests that an individual should depart well rested, depart during daylight, rest upon arrival, not eat excessively while traveling.

Books

How not to train

By ED BURKE

Put this down as Burke's first law of cycling: Never copy the training programs of champions.

Why not? Because you never know whether the guy's a champion because of or in spite of what he is doing. Nevertheless, it is fun to jump into a good argument about training methods.

In talking with many coaches and cyclists, I have become convinced that a good number of training programs are followed mainly because so-and-so (fill in your favorite champion) had great success with the method. Explore this path of investigation and you will soon discover that everything and anything has made a champion.

Trial and error has brought the art of training a long way and I don't want to discount the value of experience, either one's own or that of champions. But my point is that the science of training has developed quite far and can provide the kind of reasonable direction a cyclist needs.

The demands of the racing event and the demands of the human body are no mystery. A little knowledge of exercise physiology can help you know how to train more efficiently for what you want your body to do. For this reason, I am going to point you toward your nearest library or bookstore to do a little reading. I hope that after some study you will be confident in knowing *how* to train, not just how *they* train.

Physiology of Exercise for Physical Education and Athletics by **Herbert A. deVries. Wm. C. Brown Co. Publishers, 1974.**

The author has made an effort to bring theory and practice into a closer and more meaningful relationship. The book tells how to approach training, as well as the reasons for doing it in the manner recommended. The author assumes that the cyclist has very little background in physiology.

Human Physiology by **Vander, Sherman, Luciano. McGraw-Hill Book Company, 1970.**

This book presents the fundamental mechanisms of human physiology. It is intended for athletes with little or no scientific training; it aims to tell a story, not write an encyclopedia. Though not an exercise physiology book, it contains excellent chapters on such topics as muscle, respiration and circulation.

Science and Sport by **Vaughn Thomas. Little, Brown and Company, 1970.**

Since this book is intended for a non-technical audience, the author has adopted a personal style of writing and avoided formal textbook terminology. Thomas recommends dozens of specific exercises for developing strength, speed and stamina, and gives a wealth of advice on the learning and training methods for any sport, from weight lifting and distance running to cycling. This book is a paperback and costs about $3.

Scientific Basics of Athletic Conditioning by Jensen and Fisher. Lea and Febiger Company, 1972.

This book provides a simple, understandable introduction to physiology and anatomy. The cyclist will benefit from segments on the development of traits basic to performance, the influence of conditioning and performance, and conditioning for specific activities. The author takes a brief look at the effects of altitude, nutrition, and ergogenic aids on conditioning and performance.

Textbook of Work Physiology by Astrand and Rodahl. McGraw-Hill Book Company, 1970.

This is another excellent book, although it assumes that the reader has an elementary background in chemistry, anatomy and physiology. To help you understand some of the physiological and biochemical changes that occur during exercise, a certain amount of basic physiology and biochemistry has been included. This text is considered by many to be the bible of exercise physiology.

New sports medicine books valuable to cyclists

By ED BURKE

Many books about sports medicine and nutrition have come onto the market recently. I've had a chance to go through several and to come up with my opinions on their value to racing cyclists and coaches.

The Sports Medicine Book by Gabe Mirkin and Marshall Hoffman, 225 pages, $6.95. Boston: Little, Brown and Company, 1978.

Many individuals have been attracted to bicycle racing in the past several years. The methods of training are as varied as the athletes taking part. Unfortunately, the number of injuries and discomforts that can accompany exercise are just as numerous. In many cases the discomforts are a result of people not understanding their bodies and their exercise.

This book is an excellent guide to many sports topics, but most importantly to common injuries. It tells what to do for them, who to see for them, and how to prevent them. The book is perfect for the layman because the numerous topics are covered in a short, concise manner and with practical application to the cyclist.

Toward an Understanding of Human Performance edited by Edmund J. Burke, 92 pages, $7.50. Ithaca, NY: Movement Publications, 1977.

The 26 articles by 24 different authors include nine that are reprinted from other publications. The general quality of the articles is high, and the coverage of aspects of human performance in sports is good.

The first eight chapters deal with the components of physical fitness and how human performance is improved by training. Three chapters are devoted to nutrition and weight control, and three discuss special aspects of women's training. There are chapters on warm-up, heat stress and fluid balance, as well as the physical requirements of many different sports. The book is valuable to individuals wishing to learn the training methods of other sports.

Sports Physiology by Edward L. Fox, 383 pages, $11.95. Philadelphia: W. B. Saunders Co., 1979.

With emphasis on application to sports rather than to physiology, this text is excellent for coaches and cyclists. The concise presentation incorporates the most recent research findings wherever applicable.

The contents include such valuable topics as the fuel for exercise, the recovery process, methods and effects of weight resistance training, and sprint and endurance training. Plus much more. The appendices have questions and answers on the text material, and the glossary will be a valuable addition to any racing cyclist. Many references are cited concerning literature relevant to cycling.

Nutritional Aspects of Human Physical and Athletic Performance by Melvin H. Williams, 444 pages, $16.95. Springfield, IL: Charles C. Thomas, 1977.

A comprehensive and up-to-date book on nutrition for human performance has finally been written. Dr. Williams has combed the world's literature for the significant research related to this complex and difficult topic, and he has produced an authoritative and highly readable summary of the available information.

He deals with the basic concepts of exercise metabolism and the production of energy. He looks into the sources of energy and the particular role of each, including the role of water and electrolytes during exercise. He concludes with the specific problems of feeding the athlete. Along the way he discusses and wipes out food faddism and nutritional quackery.

It's an absolute must for every cyclist interested in nutrition.

The Physiology and Biomechanics of Cycling by Irvin E. Faria and Peter R. Cavanagh, 179 pages, $9.95. New York: John Wiley & Sons, 1978.

Bridging the gap between scientific studies and practical application, this book provides the basics for understanding the physiological and biomechanical aspects of cycling. The authors discuss: 1. energy systems and their use during cycling of various durations and intensities; 2. practical approaches to scientifically sound training techniques; 3. primary muscle action during cycling; 4. forces that affect cycling performance; 5. data relating to age and sex of cyclists. This book is valuable for serious racers and coaches.

Cycling Physiology for the Serious Cyclist by Irvin E. Faria, 162 pages, $10.95. Springfield, IL: Charles C. Thomas, 1978.

This is a watered down version of the preceding work. Three chapters in this book which would be of added interest are: 1. Muscle Fiber Type and Training; 2. Weight Training for the Cyclist; and 3. Cycling Energetics. Each chapter is well referenced and cyclists looking for technical research articles on their sport will find this book very useful.

In short, Faria's second book contains much advice. But if you are on a limited budget the first one would be the better choice.

Nutrition and Athletic Performance by Ellington Darden, 208 pages, $4.95. Pasadena, CA: The Athletic Press, 1976.

If you're interested in improving your nutritional status as well as your cycling performance, you'll find Dr. Darden's book contains sensible answers to all your questions. It is based on scientific, proven facts rather than myths and whims. Darden, who has a Ph. D. in physical education, did postdoctoral work in nutrition at Florida State.

The book is written in a question-and-answer format and covers many of the ins and outs of nutrition. An excellent chapter on food and exercise for the female athlete is included. This book is highly recommended for all cyclists, coaches and trainers who wish to become more enlightened concerning nutrition and athletic performance.

Eating to Win: Food Psyching for the Athlete by Frances Goulart, 237 pages, $8.95. New York: Stein and Day, 1978.

Reading this book is bound to make any sensible cyclist nauseous. If you believe everything in it you won't know whether to drink a cup of ginseng before a road race or rely on brewers yeast in a raw honey potion. Why can't a cyclist rely on honest training and a sound diet to get psyched up?

Goulart seems to base much of her ideas on the knowledge of such well known nutritionists as Joe Namath and Billie Jean King. If you want to develop sound nutritional practices, you should opt for the less sensational but sound findings of Williams or Darden.

The Complete Diet Guide for Runners and Other Athletes **edited by Hal Higdon, 235 pages, $4.95.**

Mountain View, CA: World Publications, 1978.

An excellent book containing 21 chapters which cover topics from athletic drinks and carbohydrate loading to vitamin supplements and vegetarianism. What makes it good is that most chapters are written by experts who know their topic well. One exception is the chapter on Nathan Pritikin's Diet (Longevity Research Institute, Santa Barbara, CA) by Donald Monkerud.

The book is loaded with helpful illustrations, graphs and tables. Without a doubt this book and Dr. Darden's are excellent values for their modest price.